The Philip Rapp Joke File
The Best Yucks from a Hollywood Gagster

by Philip Rapp

Foreword by Gary Owens
Edited by Ben Ohmart

The Philip Rapp Joke File: The Best Yucks from a Hollywood Gagster
By Philip Rapp

© 2007 Paul Rapp for the Philip Rapp Estate

Foreword © 2007 Gary Owens
Editor's Note © 2007 Ben Ohmart

All rights reserved.

No part of this book may be reproduced in any form or by any means, electronic, mechanical, digital, photocopying or recording, except for the inclusion in a review, without permission in writing from the the publisher.

www.BearManorMedia.com
1-800-566-1251 (Order line only)

ISBN10: 1-59393-102-6
ISBN13: 978-1-59393-102-5

Printed in the United States

Book Cover Design & Typesetting by SUN Editing & Book Design,
www.suneditwrite.com

Published in the USA by Bear Manor Media
PO Box 71426
Albany, GA 31708

For my lovely wife Mayumi
Sweet, supportive, fun and funny

Welcome to The Hallowed Pages of Phil Rapp's Gag File!

PHIL WAS A HIGHLY REGARDED COMEDY WRITER with many accomplishments—including *The Eddie Cantor Show* & *The Bickersons*. Rocky Kalish, a great writer for *F-Troop*, *All in the Family* and *Too Close for Comfort* told me, "Phil was responsible for one of the most noted radio shows in the history of broadcasting. My father, who did not laugh at anything, would fall down listening to The Bickersons." Rocky and his talented wife Irma just received doctorates from Syracuse University!

Legendary producer and comedy writer for the Oscars (for 50 years), Hal Kanter says, "Y'know, I was always impressed by Phil's work." Hal was a writer for so many Bob Hope and Bing Crosby films.

Paul Pumpian, who scribed for Milton Berle and Pat Buttram, told me, "Phil Rapp was truly one of the great students of comedy." Incidentally, Paul and I were two of the writers of the best-selling comedy book of the 1960s, *Elephants, Grapes & Pickles*.

This volume from Ben Ohmart's fine publishing company BearManor Media will give you a nifty cross-section of Rapp's voluminous joke file — my sister would plotz while listening to The Bickersons, so our whole family loved Phil's sillies!

I started kreebling comedy in cartoons when I was a teenager! When I came to Hollywood — I became a writer for Jay Ward Productions: *Rocky & Bullwinkle, The Nut House, Fractured Flickers*. Later: funnies for *The Alan Thicke Show, The Jim Nabors Show, Rowan & Martin's Laugh-In, Letters to Laugh-In, The Gong Show*, plus hosting a daily national radio show for 35 years …

(Clutching my security blanket, which suffers from hypertension) I've been an integral part of companies which included Mel Blanc, Pat McCormick (*The Tonight Show*), John Rappaport (producer of *MASH*), Albert Brooks and Jonathan Winters! That's why you should heed my words.

So look over these chuckles from the talented Phil Rapp:

And listen to the mating call of the duck-billed platitude! With jokes sung so clearly you can understand every worb!

Best to you—

Gary Owens
Friend of those who want no friends!

Editor's Note

When I was 10 years old, I discovered old-time radio via a set of comedy tapes in Waldenbooks. I think the four tapes included were Fibber McGee & Molly, Amos 'n' Andy, Jack Benny, and The Bickersons. I liked them all, in VArying degrees, but to my mind, the most consistently brilliant writing came from Philip Rapp's version of marital poison, The Bickersons, starring Don Ameche and Frances Langford. Little did I realize that years later I would not only write the official book on The Bickersons and edit two volumes of Bickersons scripts, but count Phil's son Paul Rapp as a good friend.

Few writers are given the opportunity I was: total access to a comedy writer's infinite output. More than 20 boxes of material—scripts, notes, ideas, more scripts; including Phil's complete joke file, which he used to spice up the likes of scripts for Eddie Cantor, Danny Kaye, Fanny Brice, Frank Morgan, and of course, Don Ameche and Frances Langford. As soon as I saw the joke file, I knew it would make a great book. I'm sure you'll agree.

The jokes were typed (rarely handwritten) on index cards, one card per joke, divided into sections (Marriage, Money, Health, etc.). There were a lot of repetitions and variations of situations. For the sake of reader clarity, I didn't use everything that Phil wrote. After all, we're talking about more than 10,000 jokes/gags/dialogues, some of which are dated, either through reference (such as using Jean Harlow as a punchline; but Phil doesn't resort to this often), or which audiences today would just find plain offensive. It was a different world 70 years ago.

Some jokes and whole subjects I didn't dare put in this collection, *but*—here are some great examples:

> "I vent blackberrying today."
> "You did?"
> "Yah, I vent to a colored funeral."

Under the category of HEAVEN, we get this vastly politically-incorrect example:

> A colored man and a Hebrew both died. When the
> colored man came to the heavenly gates, St. Peter said

he could wish for anything he wanted, so the colored man wished for a million dollars, and St. Peter gave it to him. St. Peter: "I suppose you wish for a million dollars also?" "No," answered the Hebrew, "all I want is fifty dollars worth of fake jewelry and an hour alone with the colored man."

And under the LAZINESS category:

"You're too lazy to be a valet. You're the slowest valet I ever had! Aren't you quick at anything?"
"Yowz-ah! Nobody kin git tired as fast as I can."

And

Two Hebrews were walking up Broadway in New York one day. One says, "Abie, I vish I owned dat big building." His friend says, "If you did would you gif me half?" Abie says, "No, I vouldn't, you make your own vishes."

There was an entire IRISH section as well, with jokes like:

"Why are ye decoratin' ye flat, Mrs. Clandy?"
"My b'y Danny is comin' home today."
"I t'ought he wuz sent up for foive years."
"He wuz; but he got a year off for good behavior."
"Sure—an' it must be a great comfort to ye to have a good boy like that!"

Plus,

"Yez be worrukin night and day."
"Yis, Oi'm under bonds to keep this pace for pulling the hair of that blaggard, Mrs. Murphy; and the judge told me if Oi ever touched her agin' he would fine me ten dollars."
"And yez is worrukin so hard to kape out of mischief?"
"No, O'im savin' oop the fine."

And the delightfully un-PR:

An Irishman in New York says he isn't going to have any more children (he has a family of four) as he read where every fifth child born in New York is a Jew.

"Liza, you've been brought in for intoxication."
"Dat's fine, Judge. When does we start?"

Then there are jokes with punchlines difficult for modern audiences to discern these days, since language has changed:

"I'm savin' up for a little home for you."
"I'll give you something toward it right now—the gate!"

Some gags ended up in Bickersons routines, and other interesting places. Whether or not Rapp originated them or sold them as individual jokes is impossible to tell. This appeared in one form on an Abbott and Costello radio show:

"Here's to the greatest gambler of all times—Lady Godiva. She put everything she had on a horse."

Philip Rapp was certainly one of the most gifted radio comedy writers around, and went on to invade television (*Topper, The Adventures of Hiram Holiday*) and films (*The Inspector General, The Secret Life of Walter Mitty*), but perhaps his greatness legacy is simply the radio gag. The wit was bright, snappy and sliced like a box cutter. Enjoy!

Ben Ohmart
April 2007

ABSENT-MINDEDNESS

No wonder a hen gets discouraged—she can never find things where she lays them.

ACCIDENTS

"Poor old Jack was sure out of luck … he had his head shot off just after he'd finished shaving."

"Tell me, what's the matter with me?"
"You were bit by a dog."
"What kind of a dog?"
"A mad dog."
"What, he bit me and he's mad now?"

"In New York there is a man run over every ten minutes."
"What a man—what a man!"

Extract from a newspaper account of an accident: "The accident bruised her somewhat and hurt her otherwise."

"I've got to get rid of my chauffeur; he's nearly killed me four times."
"Oh, give him another chance."

"Last summer I almost had my hand taken off at the wrist—by an axe."
"That's nothing. Last night I had my hand taken off at the knee—by a woman."

"I hear they had a fire at your hotel. They tell me you barely escaped."
"Not exactly—I had my pajamas on."

"How did you meet with this accident?"
"It wasn't an accident—a dog bit me."
"Well, don't you call that an accident?"
"Of course not, he did it on purpose."

"Mrs. Jones, who lost her thumb in the railroad accident, has recovered $10,000 damages."
"Why was her thumb so valuable?"
"It was the one she kept her husband under."

"I gave that man 50 cents for saving my life."
"What did he do?"
"He gave me thirty cents change."

"When the elevator fell with you, I suppose all your sins flashed before your eyes?"
"Well, we only dropped three stories!"

"Have you ever been in an automobile accident?"
"Well, I met my husband in a garage."

"Why're you stopping, man? You can't park here."
"I've got a flat tire, officer. I ran over a bottle about a mile back."
"Couldn't you see it and drive around it?"
"No, the damn fool had it in his hip pocket."

"The man you ran over with your car the other day is out of danger."
"That's good."
"He died this morning."

"What's wrong, Pat?"
"I burnt my hand in the hot water."
"Serves you right! Why didn't you feel the water before you put yer hand in?"

"You admit you drove over this man with a loaded truck?"
"Yes, your honor."
"And what have you to say in your defense?"
"I didn't know it was loaded!"

ACTORS

"My dear girl, I wish you would wear a different gown in the second act."
"But, Mr. Producer, this is the latest style, and I paid two hundred dollars for it."
"That may be true, but when your husbands says, 'Woman, you are hiding something from me,' the audience can't figure out what he means."

"Oh, I know I'm not a star. But I do think that my name should be featured. Why don't you mention the name of the show plus the principals, and then before my name put AND, not BUT!"

"What's the matter with the leading lady?"
"She only got nine bouquets of flowers."
"Good Heavens! Isn't that enough?"
"Nope, she paid for ten."

"So your great Russian actor was a total failure?"
"Yes. It took all our profits to pay for running the electric sign with his name on it."

"Wake up, critic! How can I get your opinion when you are asleep?"
"Sleep, my boy, is an opinion."

"Is he a ham actor?"
"No—you can *cure* ham."

"How did you like that impersonation of you I gave?"
"Well, I'll tell you—one of us is *lousy*."

"If you want me at all, you'd better put me on the payroll right now. There are several other companies after me."
"Yes? What companies?"
"Electric, light and gas."

"I came near being an actor once."
"How was that?"
"I had my leg in a cast."

ADVERTISEMENTS

This is the kind of a want ad that draws: "The ladies of the Orange Street Church have discarded clothes of all kinds. Call at 222W Orange Street and inspect them."

"I saw an ad last week offering a pocket fire escape for five dollars. So I sent for it."
"What did you receive?"
"A small Bible."

"Wanted: a salesgirl. Must be respectable, till after Christmas."

"For sale: folding bed by a lady that doubles up and looks like a piano."

"Wanted: small apartment by couple with no children until May 1st."

ADVICE

"I've walked to school twice with Ruth, bought her ice cream three times and soda once. Now, ought I to kiss her?"
"Naw, you've done enough for that girl."

"You ought to keep your eyes open around here today."
"Why?"
"Because you'll look like an idiot with them shut."

"That guy sure was fresh! But take my advice. Never slap a guy when he's chewing tobacco."

"Never strike a woman. Just tell her how pretty she *used* to be."

"What are you feeling blue about?"
"I'm dead broke. Just one penny, that's every cent I have in the world."
"Well, I'll tell you what to do. You take that penny and swallow it, then go to a doctor and tell him what you've done."
"What good will that do?"
"Oh, he'll make you cough up at least three dollars."

AGE

"My sister was celebrating with a big party last night."
"What was the celebration?"
"She was celebrating the tenth anniversary of her thirtieth birthday."

"How old are you?"
"I have seen sixteen summers, sir."
"How long have you been blind?"

"Is Alice shy about telling her age?"
"Very—about ten years shy."

"I'm thirty, Your Honor."
"You've given that age in this court for the last three years."
"You want me to change my testimony?"

"Don't you think she is older than she makes out?"
"Well, she's not as young as she makes up."

"How old are you, my little man?"
"Nine."
"And what are you going to be?"
"Ten."

ANCESTORS

"Fred, at times you seem to be manly enough, and then at others times you are absolutely effeminate."
"That's because half of my ancestors were men and the other half were women."

"No one understands me. As an old friend of the family, can you tell me why?"
"Your mother was a telephone operator and your father was a train announcer."

ANIMALS

"Is this a pedigree dog?"
"I should say he is. Why, if he could talk, he wouldn't speak to either of us."

"Is Fido a good watch dog?"
"Is he? Why, our house was robbed three times and Fido watched intently."

"Do you mind dogs in here?"
"Yes, we do."
"Well, will you please mind mine for a few minutes?"

"Poor little chamelion. Tommy put him on a Scotch plaid skirt and it burst itself trying."

"Is that pooch a bird dog?"
"Sure—c'mere, Oscar, and give the lady the bird."

"The horse I was riding wanted to go one way and I wanted to go the other."
"Who won?"
"He tossed me for it."

"My best hen simply laid herself to death."
"Died from ova-work, you might say."

"What is it that lives in a stall, eats oats, and can see equally at both ends?"
"I don't know."
"A blind horse."

"My dog has one bad habit. He eats a heavy meal in the dining room then goes into the parlor and regrets it."

"My dog took the first prize at the cat show."
"How?"
"He took the cat."

"I understand the language of wild animals."
"Well, the next time you see a skunk, ask him what's the big idea!"

"Does your dog chase cows?"
"No, he's a bull dog."

(Looking at an orangutan in a zoo) "Doesn't it look like uncle?"
"Hush, you mustn't say such things."
"But it doesn't understand, does it?"

"So you own a pet store? Do you have any trouble selling parrots?"
"Oh no, they speak for themselves."

"Mamma, where do elephants come from?"
"Why, er—"
"Come now—don't tell me that one about the stork again."

"Do you want to sell that horse?"
"Sure, I'll sell him," said the farmer.
"Can he run?" asked the young man.
"Can he run?" The farmer stepped up to the horse, slapped him smartly on the hindquarters and off trotted the horse at full speed, running just as prettily as could be. The young man thought he had never seen a prettier horse. Suddenly, the horse ran full speed into a tree.
"Is he blind?" asked the young man quickly.
"Hell no," the farmer replied. "He just don't give a damn!"

Some noisy relatives were visiting a couple, and happened to mention their dog, a big mongrel. "He's just like one of the family," said one. "Which one?" asked the hostess.

"If a number of sheep is called a herd, and a number of cattle is called a flock, what would a number of camels be?"
"A carton."

ARGUMENTS

"Every time I have an argument with my wife, I enter it in a small diary."
"Oh, a scrap book."

"Go if you must, but you are leaving me without reason."
"I always leave things as I find them."

ARMY

"Why didn't you enlist, George?"
"I had trouble with my feet."
"Flat or cold?"

"See that drum? My grandfather used it in the Civil War."
"Yeah, I suppose he beat it when the enemy came."

"And that terrible scar, Major? Did you get it during an engagement?"
"No—the first week of our honeymoon."

"Is there much graft in the army?"
"Hell, lad, even the bayonets are fixed."

"When you were in the army, what were you? What were your duties?"
"I took care of all the twenty-five-cent pieces."
"You took care of all the twenty-five-cent pieces?"
"Yeah, I was the quartermaster."

"Jenkins, why haven't you shaved this morning?"
"Why, ain't I shaved?"
"No, you ain't, and I want to know the reason why!"

"Well, now, I guess it must be this way. There was a dozen of us using the same looking glass—and I guess I must've shaved somebody else!"

The Captain said, "Boys, I'm afraid we're in a tight spot. Fight like the devil until all your cartridges are gone and then run … I'm a little lame so I'll start now."

"Have you heard the story about the nasty military officer?"
"No, what about him?"
"He was rotten to the corps!"

"All you without arms hold up your hands!"

ARTISTS

"With a single stroke of a brush, an artist can change a smiling face into a frowning one."
"That's nothing—my mother can do that with the back of a hair brush."

"This is the best painting I have ever done."
"Don't let that discourage you."

"May I paint you in the nude?"
"I expect you to wear *something*."

"Now, I suppose that is one of those horrible portraits you call art?"
"No, madam, that's a mirror."

"Were you ever done in oil?"
"Do I look like a sardine?"

"The hand should not be longer than 11 inches."
"And why not?"
"Why, it would be a foot."

"I'd like you to paint a portrait of my late uncle."
"Bring him in."
"I said my *late* uncle."
"Well, bring him in as soon as he gets here."

"Here is one of my latest paintings. It represents a contented cow grazing on a green meadow."
"But I don't see any grass."
"Of course not. The cow has eaten the grass."
"And I don't see any cow."
"Of course not, you don't expect the cow to stay after all the grass in gone, do you?"

"I once painted a picture of a face that was so natural that I had to shave it twice a week."

"I would like to hear your candid opinion of that painting of mine."
"My dear fellow, it is absolutely worthless."
"I know, but I'd like to hear it just the same."

"I should like to specialize in miniatures."
"Why miniatures?"
"I know very little about painting."

"You say that I am the first model you ever kissed?"
"Yes."
"And how many models have you had before me?"
"Four. An apple, two oranges and a box of cigars."

"How did that statue you were working on turn out?"
"It was a bust."

"What kind of work do you do?"
"I am a painter."
"How wonderful. What do you paint?"
"Why, I paint men and women."
"Oh, you mean you paint portraits?"
"No. I paint MEN on one door and WOMEN on the other."

"This is my latest picture, and I tell you ten thousand wouldn't buy it."
"I know it, and I'm one of the ten thousand."

AUTOMOBILES

"The automobile is taking the place of the horse everywhere these days."
"Do you really think so, madam?"
"Yes, I found a piece of tire in the sausages you sold me yesterday."

"I clearly had the right of way when this man ran into me and you said I was to blame."
"You certainly was."
"Why?"
"Because his father is the mayor, his brother is the chief of police, and I'm going with his sister."

"How long did it take your wife to learn to drive?"
"It will be ten years in June."

"What do you call a man who drives a car?"
"That depends on how close he comes to me."

"I can't afford an automobile."
"But I thought you have one?"
"I have, that's how I discovered I couldn't afford one."

"Since I bought that car I don't have to walk to the bank to make my deposits."
"Of course not. You ride."
"No—I don't make any."

"How long did it take you to learn how to drive a car?"
"Oh, about three or four."
"Days?"
"No, cars."

"How did you happen to have an accident with that used car I sold you?"
"I couldn't put out my hand while I was pushing it around a corner!"

"So you were going sixty miles an hour, huh?"
"I had to, judge, I just stole the car."
"Case dismissed."

Here lies the body of William Jay,
Who died maintaining his right of way.
He was right, dead right, as he sped along,
But he's just as dead as if he'd been wrong.

"Your car is at the door, sir."
"Yes, I hear it knocking."

Take one reckless, natural-born fool; two or three drinks of bad liquor; a fast, high-powered motor car. Soak the fool in liquor, place in car and let him go. After due time, remove from wreckage, place in black satin-lined box and garnish with flowers.

"How did the accident happen?"
"My wife fell asleep in the back seat."

"The horn on this car is broken."
"No, it's not, it's just indifferent."
"What do you mean?"
"Why, it just doesn't give a hoot."

"Judge, I wasn't going forty miles an hour, nor thirty, nor even twenty."
"Here, steady now, or you'll be backing into something!"

"What is your car, a five passenger?"
"Yes, but I get in eight if they're well acquainted."

"How much will it cost to fix my car?"
"What's the matter with it?"
"I don't know."
"$48.50."

"What kind of car do you have?"
"I've got a Dawn."
"A Dawn?"
"Yes, it breaks every morning."

"They're putting false beards on Fords now."
"Why?"
"To make them look like Lincolns."

"I have had this car for a year and never had a wreck."
"You mean you've had this wreck for a year and never had a car."

"What was the greatest misfortune you ever had with a car?"
"Buying it."

BACHELORS

A bachelor is a man who never makes the same mistake once.

BALDNESS

"I suppose you carry a memento of some sort in that locket of yours?"
"Yes, it's a lock of my husband's hair."
"But your husband is still living."
"Yes, but his hair is gone."

"I hear that Jones has bought a toupee."
"Shh! He's keeping it under his hat."

BARBERS

"Now, my little man, how would you like your hair cut?"
"With a hole in the top, like dad has."

"Well, do you want a haircut? It'll cost you fifty cents."
"Why, your sign says first-class haircut twenty-five cents."
"Yes, but your hair is not first class."

BEGGARS

"What's the idea of begging with two hats?"
"Business picked up and I had to expand."

"Say, buddy, could you spare a buck for a cup of coffee?"
"A dollar for coffee? Ridiculous!"
"Just tell me yes or no—but don't try to tell me how to run my business."

"You said you were too weak from starvation to work. Now that I have given you a good meal, do you feel equal to doing a little work in return?"
"Lady, your dinner did me so much good, that I feel more than equal to work—I feel superior to it!"

BOATS

"Captain, what is a good cure for sea sickness?"
"Whenever you feel the symptoms coming on, go sit under a tree."

"Let go the anchor!"
"Why, I ain't even touched it yet."

"We've been in this sailboat a half hour and haven't moved a yard."
"That's nothing. I can run a mile and only move two feet."

BOFFS

"I heard that John, the half-man, half-woman, is sick."
"Yes, I know she hasn't been feeling himself lately."

"I don't think the biggest fool in the country could make you laugh tonight."
"Try."

"I hear that Smith refuses to speak to Jones anymore. What's the trouble?"
"Well, Jones' wife had twins and they both look like Smith."
"And Smith is sore?"
"Yeah—he wanted boys."

"Only fools are certain; wise men hesitate."
"Are you sure, dad?"
"Yes."

BOOKS

"This book will do half your work."
"Okay, then give me two of them."

"It's pretty dull," said the critic. "It would be a good thing for a soldier to wear over his heart when going to battle."
"Why?"
"Well, if a bullet struck that book, it would never get past the first chapter."

"Does this novel end happily?"
"No, they get married."

"I would like a book, please."
"Something light?"
"It doesn't matter. I have my car with me."

BORROWING

"Paw, what's the difference between capital and labor?"
"Well, the money you lend represents capital, and getting it back represents labor, my son."

"I'm surprised at you refusing to lend me five dollars. One friend should always be willing to help the other."
"I know, but you always insist on being the other."

"Has Owens ever paid back that $10 you loaned him a year ago?"
"Oh, sure. He borrowed $25 from me last week and only took $15."

A Texas tradesman has this sign in a conspicuous place in his store:
Man is made of dust.
Dust settles.
Be a man.

"The short story seems to be very popular these days."
"Yes, nearly every man I meet stops to tell me how short he is."

"I asked you to loan me a hundred dollars, and you let me have only fifty."
"That's fair enough, isn't it? I lose fifty, and you lose fifty."

"Mr. Jones, Father wants to borrow your paper, he only wants to read it."
"Well, go back and tell your father to send me his supper ... tell him I only want to eat it."

"I am going to pay you back the money I owe you in a few weeks."
"Why, you don't owe me anything."
"I will in a few minutes."

BRAVERY

"Once I saved a man's life, but I never got a medal for it."
"How did you save his life?"
"A drunk once came home to his apartment and turned on only the hot water to take a bath in, and he would have been scalded to death—only I happened to be the janitor of the building and there was no hot water."

BUSINESS

"Why is it that Jews don't go to heaven anymore?"
"Why?"
"Because business has gone to hell."

The cost of living is slightly higher than it was a year ago. This is because there is such a demand for it.

"What business is your brother in?"
"My brother, Gus, has gone into real estate."
"So, Gus has gone into real estate, eh?"
"Yes, we buried him last week."

"You're taking a business course?"
"Yes. I'm learning the touch system."
"Typewriting, eh?"
"No, loans and mortgages."

"How's business?"
"Bad! Even the people who never pay me have stopped buying!"

CHEATING

"Yesterday I caught my wife kissing the milkman. This morning I caught her kissing the iceman. What shall I do?"
"Be patient, it may be your turn next."

"Sarah, we've got to move out of here right away. I just found out the most terrible thing. The janitor of this house is going around boasting that he has kissed every woman in the house except one."
"I know, it's that stuck-up Mrs. Rosenbaum on the third floor."

"What became of your valet?"
"I fired him for removing a spot from my dress suit."
"That was part of his duty."
"Yes, but this was a five spot."

CHILDREN

"So God has sent you two more brothers, eh, little boy?"
"Yes, and He knows where the money is coming from—I heard Daddy say so."

"Mother, let me go to the zoo to see the monkeys."
"Why, Tim, what an idea! Imagine, wanting to go see the monkeys in the zoo when your Aunt Betsy is here!"

"What are you crying for, my little man?"
"My father and mother's fighting ..."
"Oh, that's too bad. Who is your father?"
"That's what they're fighting about."

"What's the matter, little boy?"
"Please sir, have you seen a lady without a little boy who looks like me?"

"What's the matter, little boy?"
(Crying) "Maw drowned all the kittens."
"Dear me. That's too bad."
"Yeah, an' she promised me I could do it ...!"

"Why did you buy a dachshund for the children?"
"So they can all pet him at once."

"Why use such a high crib for your baby?"
"So we can hear him when he falls out."

"Your boy just threw a stone at me."
"Did he hit you?"
"No."
"Then it wasn't my boy."

"Why are you crying, little fellow?"
"We've got chicken and pie for dinner …"
"Well, that's nothing to cry about."
"I know, but I can't find my way home."

"That kid is certainly spoiled."
"No, they all smell like that."

"Uh oh—the baby swallowed the matches! What shall I do?"
"Here—use my cigarette lighter."

"Ma, did the Missionary say that savages didn't wear any clothes?"
"Yes, Harold."
"Then why did Pa put a button in the missionary box?"

"The thrashing I am about to give you, son, hurts me more than it will you."
"Well, don't be too rough on yourself, Pa, I ain't worth it."

"We've got a new baby at our house."
"Zat so? Who brung it?"
"Old Doc McGowan."
"We take from him, too."

"What did they teach you at school today?"
"Not much. I've got to go again …"

"Johnny, the next time you are absent I want you to bring me an excuse from your father telling me why you were not here."
"I don't want to bring an excuse from my father."
"Why not?"
"Coz he isn't any good at making excuses."

"Do you know why the little chickens come out of the eggs, dear?"
"Course I do. They knew they'd get boiled if they stayed in."

"Go right on with your piano lesson, if you're sure your hands are quite clean."
"Oh, that's all right, Miss Emily, I'm just playing on the white keys."

"Sonny doesn't believe in the old stories anymore, does he?"
"No. He won't even believe that storks bring baby storks."

"God gives us our daily bread, don't he?"
"Yes, sonny."
"And Santa Claus brings the presents?"
"Yes, dear."
"And the stork brings the babies?"
"That's right, dear."
"Then tell me, Ma, what's the use of having Papa hang around?"

"My father's a doctor. I can be sick for nothing."
"Well, mine's a preacher … so I can be good for nothing."

"Don't you find that a new baby brightens up a home wonderfully?"
"Yes, we have the lights on all through the night now."

"Why are you crying, little boy?"
"I just had the measles and had to cut school for a month."
"Well, never mind, you can't get them again."
"That's why I'm cryin'!"

(Saying his prayers) "And please make Cyril stop throwing stones at me. By the way, I've mentioned this before."

"The minister is going to be here for dinner and you must have your face washed before he comes."
"Yeah, and suppose he don't come? What then?"

Little Brother: "I've got an idea. I think if I left the room you'd kiss sister."
Big Sister: "Bobby, how dare you say such a thing! Leave the room immediately."

"Willie, I wish you would run across the street and see how old Mrs. Brown is this morning."
"Yes, ma'am." Later: "Mrs. Brown says it's none of your business how old she is."

"I do wish that Santa Claus brought me a new doll for Christmas."
"But your old doll is as good as ever."
"So am I as good as ever, but the doctor brought you a new baby!"

"Mama, why has papa no hair?"
"Because he thinks so much, dear."
"Then why do you have so much?"

"What is your father's name?"
"Daddy."
"Has he no other name?"
"No."
"Then what does your mother call him?"
"Fathead."

"Willie, go in and kiss the new nurse and get acquainted."
"What, and get a sock in the jaw like papa did?"

"Dad, can you still do tricks?"
"What do you mean, do tricks?"
"Well, Mom said you used to drink like a fish."

"How many fingers have you?"
"Ten."
"Well, if four were missing, what would you have then?"
"No music lessons!"

"Grandpa, did you ever play football?"
"Why, no, son, of course not."
"That's funny. Dad said we could get a new car when you kicked off."

"Johnny, I'd like to go through a whole day without once scolding or punishing you."
"Well, Dad, you have my consent."

"Now, my son, tell me why I punished you."
"Well, if that ain't the limit! Slap me around an' don't even know why you did it!"

"Mother, can the new maid see in the dark?"
"Why, I don't see how she could."
"Well, she told Daddy last night in the hallway that he needed a shave."

"My dad is an Elk, a Lion and a Moose."
"What does it cost to see him?"

"Do you think that you can predict a boy's future by his hobbies when he's young?"
"Certainly. My boy has a hobby of saving old magazines."
"And so you think he will be a journalist?"
"Oh, no; a dentist."

"We're goin' to move soon, Tommy."
"How do you know?"
"Mother seen me break a window and she didn't say nothin'."

"So this is the baby, eh? I used to look like him when I was his age. What's he crying about now?"
"Oh, Uncle Gust, he heard what you said!"

"While you were gone, ma'am, the baby swallowed a bug."
"Good heavens!"
"But don't worry, ma'am, I made him eat some insect powder."

"Would you mind making a noise like a frog, Uncle?"
"Why?"
"Because whenever I ask Daddy to buy me anything, he always says, 'Wait till your Uncle croaks.'"

CHURCHES

"My cousin was in church three times. The first time, they threw water on him. The second time, they threw rice on him, and the third time, they threw dirt over him."

"Our church has such a small congregation that every time our rector says 'Dearly Beloved' you feel as if somebody was proposing to you."

"Big crowd at our church last night."
"New minister?"
"No, it burned down."

Little girl: "Oh yes, I always say a prayer, like all the rest, just before the sermon begins. 'Now I lay me down to sleep …'"

"Did you enjoy your visit to that new church?"
"Nope, I never sleep well the first time in a strange place."

"Can you tell me who made you, Joe?"
"God made part of me."
"What do you mean?"
"He made me really little, and I just growed the rest myself."

CLIMATE

"What is mostly raised in damp climates?"
"Umbrellas."

"I hear you are going into business out west."
"Yes, I'm going to open a store in Arizona."
"In Arizona! Why, you can't stand it out there. It is a hundred and ten in the shade all the time."
"Well, I don't have to stand in the shade, do I?"

COLLEGE

"At first he liked being initiated—but then he got sore in the end."

"Did your son learn anything at college?"
"Nothing but card tricks."
"Card tricks?"
"Yes—about all he can do is make the jack disappear."

"Will your people be surprised when you graduate?"
"No, they've been expecting it for several years."

"So your son has his B.A. and his M.A.?"
"Yes, but his P A still supports him."

CONCEIT

"Last night I dreamed I married the most beautiful woman in the whole world."
"Were we happy?"

"I'm sorry you think I'm conceited."
"Well, no, I wouldn't say that, but I think you suffer a little from I strain."

"Dot says her face is her fortune."
"She doesn't pay much income tax, does she?"

"Sometimes I do not agree with your opinions. You can't expect to be right every time."

COOKING

"What will I get if I cook a dinner like this for you every day this year?"
"My life insurance."

"Isn't there something wrong with this cake you baked, dear?"
"No, it must be your taste. The cookbook says it's delicious."

"Do you find it more economical to do your own cooking?"
"Certainly. Since I've been doing the cooking, my husband only eats half what he used to."

COURTROOM

"Are you trying to show contempt for this court?"
"On the contrary, I'm trying hard to conceal it."

"What's the charge, officer?"
"Fragrancy, your Honor. He's been drinking perfume."

"What's your name, occupation, and what's the charge?
"My name is Sparks, I am an electrician, and I am charged with battery."
"Put this guy in a dry cell."

"It seems to me that I've seen you before."
"You have, your Honor. I'm the man that taught your daughter how to play the piano."
"Thirty years!"

"Your Honor, I plead for the dismissal of the defendant … he's deaf."
"Not granted. He'll have his hearing in the morning."

They say that gangsters use high-powered cars just to keep up disappearances.

"Justice! Justice! I demand justice!"
"Silence! The defendant will remember that he is in a courtroom."

"I caught this guy stealing bananas off a fruit stand."
"Ah! Impersonating an officer, eh? Two years."

"We just caught a woman shoplifting."
"What did she take?"
"Fifty yards of elastic."
"Well—tell her she's in for a long stretch."

"Prisoner, have you anything to offer in your own behalf?"
"No, your Honor—I turned every cent I have over to my lawyers and a couple of jurymen."

DANCING

"I hear you confessed your love to Harry while you were dancing with him. Was he surprised?"
"Yes—it swept him right off my feet!"

DEATH

"Poor old Joe is dead."
"What did he die from?"
"Cracked ice."
"Cracked ice?"
"Yes, it was on a pond."

"My uncle was finally put to rest last week."
"Why, I didn't know he had passed away."
"He didn't—but my aunt did."

"Did you know that Harold has died? Such a clever man. He knew four dead languages."
"Well, he can use them now."

DEBTS

"I just got a check from home."
"Then pay me the five bucks you owe me."
"Wait … I haven't told you the rest of the dream yet."

"Pardon me, Mr. Syp. But when may I hope to receive that five you owe me?"
"Always."

DEPRESSION

"The battle against depression has been won."
"Then why don't the employers cease firing?"

JONES: (Reading from the Society Page) "'Miss Van Der Punk will be married at noon today to Mr. John Bascombe in St. Stephen's church' — that's only two blocks from here."
CHILDREN: "Hurrah! Rice for supper!"

In some of the poorer areas of the city, life is like a game of chess—nothing but pawn, pawn, pawn.

"Last year I spent my vacation in Florida on the sands."
"And where are you going to spend it this year?"
"On the rocks."

DETECTIVES

"They say there are very few female detectives."
"That's not surprising—how would you like to be called a plain-clothes woman?"

DIVORCE

"Don't divorce your wife. Give her an automobile. The shock will kill her and you can use the machine for her funeral."

"Maud has made some fine marriages, but divorced all her husbands."
"Yeah, she moves in the best triangles."

"I want to find out if I have grounds for divorce."
"Are you married?"
"Of course I am."
"Then you have."

"I dreamed I went to hell. Beautiful golf courses. No balls."

DREAMS

"Last night I dreamed you loved me. What does that mean?"
"It was just a dream."

"I went to bed last night and dreamed that I died."
"I suppose the heat woke you up?"

"Did I tell you about the nightmare I had last night?"
"You don't have to. I've seen her with you."

DOCTORS

"I had a lady whose spine—"
"Stop! I don't want to hear any of your back talk."

"I operated on him for appendicitis."
"What was the matter with him?"

"So I've got to have an anesthetic? How long will it be before I know anything?"
"Now don't expect too much of the anesthetic."

"Let me give you something for that cough."
"You can have it for nothing."

"Is there no hope for my husband, doctor?"
"I don't know—what were you hoping for?"

"Doctor, what should I do for a broken ankle?"
"Limp."

"Doctor, tell me frankly—what are my chances?"
"Don't start reading any serial stories."

"The doctor said he would examine me for twenty dollars. I said all right, go ahead, but I want ten of it if you find it."

"Doctor, can you relieve me of what I have got?"
"Oh yes, I can do that, all right, where does your pain seem to be?"
"It seems to be in my chest, it hurts to breathe."
"I'll give you something that'll stop that."

"My dear madam, you can quite put the thought out of your head that you will be buried alive. Under my treatment that would be impossible."

"Doc, I swallowed my watch, can you give me anything for it?"
"I can give you something to pass the time."

"Doctor, can you cure me of snoring? I snore so loudly I awaken myself."
"In that case, I would advise you to sleep in another room."

The doctor writes out the prescription and says, "Now, you'll have to pay $2 for this at any drugstore."
"Doctor, may I borrow the money?"
The doctor scratches out part of the writing, hands the man a quarter and says, "The part I scratched out was for your nerves."

"Are you a trained nurse?"
"Yes."
"Let me see you do some tricks."

DRINKING

A man is drunk when he feels sophisticated and can't pronounce it.

"I don't know why I was so drunk last night. I only had one glass."
"Yes, but they kept filling it up."

"How can you tell when you are drunk, drinking that stuff you're peddling around?"
"Do you see those two men over there? Well, if you drink too much of this, they'll look like four men."
"There's only one guy there."

"Why do you drink so much?"
"To drown my troubles."
"And do you succeed in drowning them?"
"No, damnit ... they can swim!"

"I found a five-dollar bill in a speakeasy tonight."
"Yeah. I smell it on your breath."

"Believe it or not, offsher, I'm hunting for a parkin' plash."
"But you haven't an automobile."
"Yesh I have. It's in the parkin' plash I'm looking for."

Synthetic gin is something which makes a man see double and feel single.

"Give me a drink of whiskey. I'm thirsty."
"You should drink milk—milk makes blood."
"I'm not blood-thirsty."

"Is Charlie drunk again?"
"No, he's just syncopated."
"Syncopated."
"Yeah—moving unevenly from bar to bar."

"I take a bottle of gin every night before I go to bed."
"What's the idea?"
"So I'll sleep tight."

"How are you?"
"I'm up against it. I lost the best part of my baggage en route."
"Did you misplace it or was it stolen?"
"Neither. The cork came out."

"Harry was held up by two men last night."
"Where?"
"All the way home."

"I hear you have a keg of beer in your room."
"Yes, I keep it to build up my strength."
"Any results?"
"Marvelous! When I first got the thing a week ago, I couldn't even move it—and now, I can roll it around the floor!"

"All this talk about liquor makes me thirsty."
"Well, I'll go get you a glass of water."
"I said thirsty … not dirty."

EATING

"What's wrong with these eggs?"
"Don't ask me. I only laid the table."

"I'm tired of eating in restaurants."
"Why not get married?"
"I am."

"When Fred and I were in Texas on our hunting trip, he shot so many quail and made me cook them that I never want to see another one—I was just quailed to death!"
"When Dick and I were up in Canada hunting, I got just the same way about goose."

"That young bride worships her husband—doesn't she?"
"Well, she places burnt offerings before him three times a day."

"Miss Wilson, do have some more pudding."
"Well, thanks. I will take some more, but only a mouthful, please."
"Emma! Fill Miss Wilson's plate!"

"What made you so late this evening?"
"I was home taking the lock off the cupboard."
"What were you taking the lock off the cupboard for?"
"The doctor told me I had to quit bolting my food."

"How would you tell a chicken's age?"
"By the teeth."
"A chicken hasn't got teeth."
"No, but I have."

"Let's toss a coin to see who pays for lunch."
"Okay! Where are we dining?"
"Er—well—let's toss a coin first."

EDUCATION

"I've never been troubled with a college education and I'm proud of my ignorance."
"You have a lot to be proud of."

"I suppose you've been through Algebra?"
"I went through at night, but couldn't see the place."

Two young fellows, roommates, were seated in the room one evening, when one of them was astonished to see the other take a perfectly blank sheet of paper, fold it, put it into an envelope, and address and stamp the envelope carefully.
"Say, what are you mailing that blank sheet of paper for?"
"I'm taking a correspondence school course and I'm cutting a class."

"What do they mean by college bread? Is it different from any other kind of bread?"
"Yes, it is a four-year loaf."

"Yes, this is a turkeze ring."
"Excuse me, the correct pronunciation of that is turkwoise."
"No, turkeze, excuse me."
"I say turkwoise."
"Well, let's go to a jeweler and ask him."
"Right."
"In order to settle a wager," said Jones to the jeweler, "would you mind telling me if the correct pronunciation of the stone in this ring is turkeze or turkwoise?"
"The correct pronunciation is *glass*."

EMPLOYMENT

"I'm looking for someone to help me forget."
"Oh, are you a disappointed lover who craves a sympathetic female?"
"No, I'm a plumber looking for an assistant."

"My father's awful smart. He's a mechanic and makes locomotives."
"That's nothing. My father's a commuter and he makes two trains every day."

"My brother is working with five thousand men under him."
"What does he do?"
"He mows the lawns in a cemetery."

"What's his business?"
"He's a panhandler."
"Panhandler?"
"Yeah. He gives facial massages."

"What sort of a fellow is he, does he work?"
"Sure, he gets money from his father."
"That's not a job."
"You're crazy—you don't know his father!"

"Are you a clock watcher?"
"No, I don't like inside work. I'm a whistle listener."

"What are you doing now?"
"I'm a cafeteria blacksmith."
"What do you mean?"
"I shoo flies."

"What are you working at now?"
"I'm a diamond cutter."
"Oh?"
"I cut the grass at the baseball field."

"I know how to settle this unemployment problem. If we put all the men in the world on one island, and all the women on another, we'd have everybody busy in no time."
"Well, what would they be doing?"
"Boat building!"

"You've been a typist for nearly all the men in this building."
"Yes … you might say I'm on my last lap."

"I can't give you a job. Can't afford any extra help just now."
"That's all right, I won't be much help."

"My father was a spy in the United States Mint."
"Hey! A mince pie!"

"Who are you working for now?"
"Same people—wife and three kids."

"Out of a job again, eh? Seems strange that you can't hold a job more than a week."
"Well, maybe I don't work such a long time at one place—but I haven't left a place yet without everybody being perfectly satisfied."

"Your son graduated last year, didn't he? What's he working at now?"
"Rare intervals."

"So your brother tried to get a government job. What is he doing now?"
"Nothing. He got the job."

"A pal of mine landed a soft job—he's in a bloomer factory now pulling down about two thousand a year."

"What have you been doing all summer?"
"I had a position in my father's office. And you?"
"I wasn't working either."

"Do you really think you are fit for hard labor?"
"Some of the best judges in the country have thought so!"

"What is your occupation?"
"It isn't an occupation, it's a pursuit—I'm a bill collector."

"I used to work in a watch factory."
"What did you do?"
"I made faces."

"I want to give this job to a man like myself. Why, I think nothing of starting to work at five o'clock in the morning!"
"I don't think much of it, either."

"I had a job keeping the water from coming over the dam; but the water went over the dam so fast that I lost the dam job!"

"Why aren't you working today?"
"Well, I work in a domino factory, and I put on the spots, and they are making double blanks today."

EXERCISE

"I'll stand on my head or bust!"
"On your head is fine."

"Let's go for a walk."
"Walk? Why a walk?"
"Doctor's orders—he told me to exercise with a dumbbell every day."

"I think I will take up horseback riding. They say it increases your social standing."
"I don't know about the social part—but it certainly will increase your standing."

"I am very fond of horseback riding."
"Do you ride alone?"
"No, I take a horse with me."

"Do you ever take any real exercise?"
"Well—last week I was out for seven nights running!"

FARM

"Those are pretty big strawberries."
"Yeah, we use a right smart heap of manure on them."
"Well, I always take sugar and cream on mine, but I say every man to his own taste."

"Oh, see that scarecrow out in the field?"
"That isn't a scarecrow."
"It must be, see how motionless it is."
"That's my farmhand."

"I've got hens that lay eggs stamped July 4th, etc."
"How do they do that?"
"I feed them a strict diet of dates."

"Why are they running a steamroller over that field?"
"They're going to raise mashed potatoes."

FIGHTING

An Arkansas man was tried for assault with intent to kill. The prosecutor produced a fence nail, an axe, a saw and a rifle, as the weapons used. The defense said that the weapons of the other man were a scythe, a pitchfork, a pistol, a razor and a hoe. The jury retired and delivered this verdict: "We, the jury, would have given a hundred dollars to have seen the fight!"

"You told me you could beat that fellow hands down!"
"But he wouldn't keep his hands down."

"Do glasses help your eyes any?"
"Do they! They kept three guys from hitting me."

"He gave me a pair of socks."
"He did? I thought he was mad at you."
"One in each eye."

"Were you injured in the fracas?"
"No, in the leg."

"Do you know that women outnumbered the men at the last prizefight I went to?"
"I guess it's the ring that attracts them."

"When I fight the champ, it'll be the battle of the century."
"Yeah—you'll never win in a hundred years!"

"Why do they always have those prizefighters roped in while they are fighting?"
"To show that they are getting the same treatment as their patrons."

"Go back and fight him, you coward."
"But he's already given me two black eyes."
"Well, he can't give you any more, can he?"

FISHING

A canny young fisher named Fisher
Once fished from the edge of a fissure
A fish with a grin
Pulled the fisherman in—
Now they are fishing the fissure for Fisher.

He had been fishing, but with bad luck. On his way back he passed a fish shop and said to the dealer, "John, stand over there and throw me five of the biggest trout you have."
"Throw 'em? What for?"
"I want to tell the family I caught them!"

This fisherman loved to fish so much he even had a catch in his voice.

"So you went fishing with Brown yesterday. How many did you catch?"
"Ask Brown. I've forgotten the number we agreed upon."

"How did you catch so many fish without using a net?"
"Well, I take the boat, go out a good ways, and then throw my chewing tobacco into the water. The fish chew the tobacco and when they come to the top to spit, I hit 'em with the oar."

"What are you going back there this summer for? Why, last year that place was full of mosquitoes and no fishing."
"The owner tells me that he has crossed the mosquitoes with the fish … and guarantees a bite every second!"

"Do fish grow very fast?"
"I should say so! Father caught one once and it grows six inches every time he mentions it."

FLIRTATION

"It's not safe to flirt with that woman. Her husband's got a title."
"Titles don't mean anything to me."
"The heavyweight title?"

"Did I tell you about the swell apartment I have here in town?"
"Well, let's not go into that."

"I hope I didn't see you smiling at that woman we just passed, John."
"I hope you didn't either."

"That girl winked her eye at me."
"What followed?"
"I did."

FOOD

"Stewed Rabbit. Is it all rabbit?"
"Not exactly, sir. A little horsemeat, too."
"Is that so? What proportion is horsemeat?"
"Fifty-fifty. One horse and one rabbit."

If you pay twenty-five cents for twenty-five cents worth of food, it's a lunch, but if you pay a dollar for twenty-five cents worth of food, it's a luncheon.

"Waiter, bring me some oysters."
"Stewed, sir?"
"None of your business."

"Hey waiter! I want to complain about this steak.
It's not tender enough!"
"Not tender enough? Do you expect it to jump up and kiss you?"

To the grocery store clerk: "Do you handle knives and forks?"
"Do I look like a man who eats with a shovel?"

"What are you selling tomatoes for today?"
"Because I have a wife and six children."

"How do you like the potato salad?"
"It's delicious—did you buy it yourself?"

"She lost her job in the grocery store because she refused to do what the boss asked of her."
"What was that?"
"He asked her to lay some eggs in the window."

"Are these eggs fresh?"
"Lady, the hen don't even know I got 'em yet."

"Did you say that you want these eggs turned over?"
"Yes, turn them over to the Museum of Natural History."

FRIENDSHIP

"Is the man who gave you that cigar one of your friends?"
"I don't know yet. I haven't smoked the cigar."

"What's the difference between an acquaintance and a friend?"
"Well, when a friend wants to borrow money, he's an acquaintance."

GOLF

"I'm not playing my usual game today, caddy."
"What's your usual game, sir? Hopscotch?"

"That was a fine drive you made this morning, dear."
"Which one do you mean?"
"Oh, you know ... that time you hit the ball."

"How is Dub getting on with his golf?"
"Pretty good ... he hit a ball in one today!"

"Pardon, but would you gentlemen mind if I played through? I just got a telegram that my wife died."

"Say, how do you address the ball?"
"You mean before I hit it—or after I lose it?"

Golf slanguage:
Golf - a chasm, the golf of Mexico
Fairway - distant, far off
Niblick - munching delicately, tasting
Green - to smile broadly
Bunker - a man who handles other people's money
Bag - to implore
Turf - tax on imports

"He was so *bad*. It wasn't a case of replacing the turf, but of returfing the place."

"My doctor says I can't play golf."
"So, he's played with you, too?"

"I know a man who once killed his wife with a golf club."
"Really? In how many strokes?"

GRAMMAR

"Johnny, give me a sentence using the pronoun 'I.'"
"I is—"
"Not 'I is,' you should say 'I am.'"
"All right—I am the ninth letter in the alphabet."

"I have went. That's wrong, isn't it?"
"Yes, ma'am."
"Why is it wrong?"
"Because you ain't went yet."

"How would you punctuate this sentence: Miss Gray a beautiful young girl of seventeen walked down the street."
"I would certainly make a dash after Miss Gray."

"What gender is cat?"
"Show me the cat."

"Give me an example of a collective noun."
"Hash!"

HEAVEN

"Hell, yes," said the Devil, picking up the telephone.

"Who are you?"
"I am a Wall Street broker."
"What do you want?"
"I want to get into heaven."
"What have you done that entitles you to admission?"
"Well, I saw a decrepit woman on Broadway the other day and gave her two cents."
"Yes, I see that marked to your credit. What else have you done?"
"Well, I crossed the Brooklyn Bridge the other night and met a newsboy half frozen to death and gave him one cent."
"What else have you done?"
"Well, I can't recollect anything else."
"Oh, here's your three cents, go to Hell!"

"Well, Clancy, here in heaven we count a million years as a minute and a million dollars as a cent."
"Ah, I'm needin' cash. Lend me a cent."
"Sure. Wait a minute."

The newcomer was playing golf in hell.
"Oh boy, what a perfect drive down the green. Where's the hole, caddy?"
"There isn't any hole, sir—that's the hell of it."

HISTORY

The greatest financier of Biblical times was Noah—because he floated alone when the rest of the world was in liquidation.

"Why was the period between A.D. 500 and A.D. 1200 known as the Dark Ages?"
"Because those were the days of Knights."

"I want to see Cleopatra."
"She is in bed with Laryngitis."
"Darn those Greeks!"

"Why don't you take Cleopatra back to Rome with you?"
"What, and let Julius Caesar?"

"In which of his battles was King Gustave Adolphus of Sweden slain?"
"His last one?"

HORSERACING

"Well, anyhow, I wasn't last. There were two horses behind me."
"They were the first two in the next race."

"The only thing that horse is fit to run against is a wall."

"And what is your name, little boy?"
"I'm Jerry Glutz, by Bill Glutz, out of Sadie Schmidt."

"Did you lose your money on fast horses?"
"No, slow ones."

In the old days if you wanted a horse to stand still, you tied him to a hitching post. Nowadays all you have to do is place a bet on him.

HOTELS

"Out in the country where I spent my vacation, they gave me one of those three season beds."
"Never heard of them."
"No Spring."

"The farmer who I was staying with had an old pig. One day the old pig died, and as a result, we ate pork for many days. He also owned an old cow. The cow died, so we had beef for weeks. Then one day his grandmother died ... so I left."

"With or without a bed?"
"With a bed?"
"I don't think I have a bed long enough for you."
"Well, I'll add two feet to it when I get in it."

"I shall have to ask you for your board in advance. Your luggage is too—er—emotional."
"Too emotional?"
"Yes—too easily moved."

"They tell me this is a good place for rheumatism."
"Oh yes, I got mine here."

"Do you want the porter to call you?"
"No, thanks, I awaken every morning at seven."
"Then would you mind calling the porter?"

ILLNESS

"I understand you were laughing during the whole operation."
"Sure, the doctor had me in stitches!"

"Where am I? Where am I? In heaven ...?"
"No dear, I'm still with you."

"Did you say you are subject to fits?"
"Yes."
"What do you do when you have one?"
"Oh, I just walk back and froth."

The man recovering from a severe operation in the hospital was *hungry*. But all he got one time a day was a teaspoonful of custard. "Is that all I get?" he asked the nurse. "That's all for a while," she said. He swallowed it with a good deal of grumbling. The nurse took away the dish, and a few minutes later was called back to the bedside by the bell. "Nurse," said the patient, "bring me a postage stamp. I want to do a little reading."

"Jones won't be out of the hospital as soon as we thought he would."
"Did you see his doctor?"
"No, I saw his nurse."

"They said I could have visitors from two to five."
"Who wants to talk to anyone that young?"

Mother to Doctor: "I think my little boy Henry has the flu. What's it worth to you if I let him go out and play with the other kids?"

"Our lodge president is going to have an operation to remove some surplus bone."
"You don't mean to tell me he is going to be beheaded?"

"Hello! How's the boy?"
"I have clothing sickness."
"What's that?"
"My tongue has a coat on it and my breath comes in short pants."

"Where have you been?"
   "In the hospital getting censored."
"Censored?"
"Yes. I had several important parts taken out."

"My wife has been enjoying poor health for the last few months, but today she is complaining of feeling better."

"You cough more easily this morning."
"I ought to, I've been practicing all night."

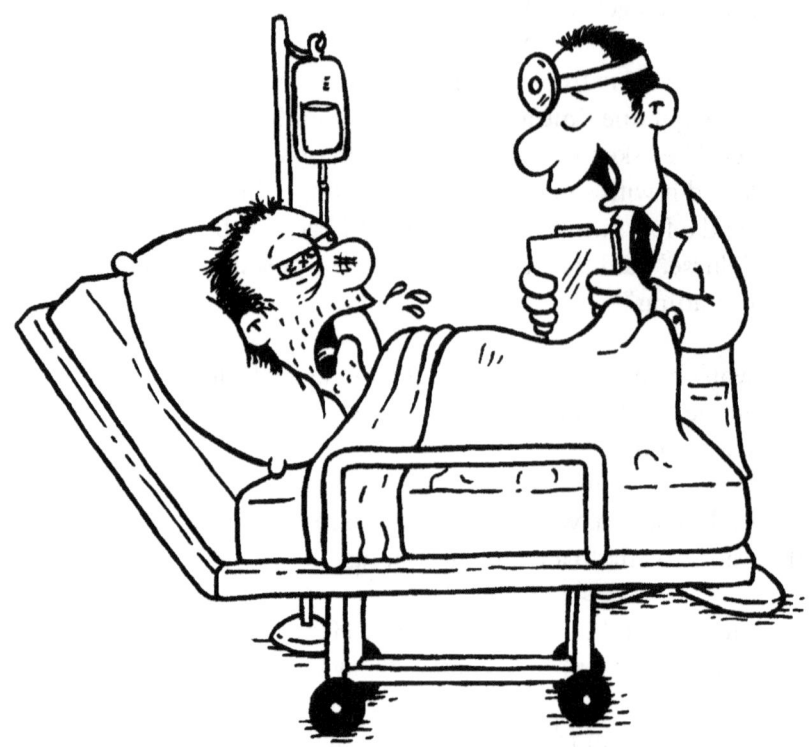

"My wife has an awful disease; kleptomania."
"Is she trying to cure it?"
"She's taking something for it."

A peculiar form of paralysis has locked a man's hands in an extended position about 37 inches apart. There is nothing he can do now except tell fish stories.

"Dear, the doctor is here to see you."
"Show him out and call the undertaker—you know I never deal with middle men."

"How did you catch such a cold?"
"Aw, somebody played the 'Star Spangled Banner' while I was taking a bath."

"Oh, doctor, I forgot to ask you about that eye medicine you gave me. Do I drop it into my eyes before or after meals?"

"Nurse, I'm in love with you—I don't want to get well."
"Don't worry, you won't. The doctor is in love with me, too—and he saw you kiss me this morning."

"I hope you are taking good care of your cold."
"You bet I am. I've had it over a week now, and it's as good as new!"

"Madam, your husband must have absolute rest."
"But doctor, he won't listen to me."
"A very good beginning, madam; an excellent beginning."

"So your uncle had an operation?"
"Yes, and we're suing the doctor."
"What for?"
"For opening my aunt's male."

"Did you hear that Jim got poisoned eating chicken?"
"Croquette?"
"Not yet, but he's pretty sick!"

"Finerty, I have a terrible toothache."
"Why don't you do what I do when I have a toothache."
"What's that?"
"I go home to me wife, she puts her arms around my neck, kisses and hugs me, smooths me forehead, and I forget all about it. Why don't ye try it?"
"I will, Finerty. Is your wife home now?"

"Nurse, have you kept a chart of his progress?"
"No, but I can show you my diary!"

There was the hospital patient who was sick for so long that every time someone knocked, he would ask, "Friend or enema?"

"My little brother Sammy swallowed a quarter and had to have an operation."
"Was the operation successful?"
"Naw, they only found eight cents."

INSANITY

A man in a mental hospital sat dangling a stick, with a piece of string attached, over a flower bed. A visitor approached and wishing to be affable, asked, "How many have you caught?" "You're the ninth," he replied.

"They say Green has been wandering in his mind for some time."
"Well, he's safe enough, he can't go far."

As a visitor to an insane asylum walked about the grounds, he noticed one of the inmates wheeling a wheelbarrow upside down. "That's no way to push that thing," said the visitor. "You've got it upside down." "Oh, have I?" answered the lunatic. "Well, I used to push it the other way and they put bricks in it."

"There's a man outside who wants to know if we have lost any of our inmates."
"Why?"
"He says that someone has run off with his wife."

INSTALLMENTS

"I've called to collect some back payments on your antique furniture."
"You're crazy. I never bought any antique furniture on the installment plan."
"Well, maybe it wasn't antique when you bought it."

"You're six payments behind on this piano."
"Well, the company advertises 'pay as you play.'"
"What's that got to do with it?"
"I play very poorly."

"Fred, the installment man is here again."
"I'll be right out—tell him to have a chair."

"So your father is ill. I hope it is nothing contagious."
"So do I. Doctor said it was from overwork."

"Yes, he had some trouble with his eyes. Every time he went to read he would read double."
"Poor fellow. I suppose that interfered with his holding a good position?"
"Not at all. The gas company gobbled him up and gave him a job reading gas meters."

INSULTS

"I have been living on my wits."
"No wonder you look so hungry."

"What donkeys we are!"
"Speak in the singular."
"Well, what an ass you are!"

"You gave me a nasty look."
"You certainly have got a nasty look, but I didn't give it to you."

"My face is my fortune."
"I hope you don't get arrested for counterfeiting."

"I have always dreaded premature burial."
"Don't worry, they can't bury you too soon."

"Is my face dirty or is it my imagination?"
"Well, your face is clean, but I don't know much about your imagination."

"You say your girlfriend is Mae West's double?"
"Yeah—she's twice her size."

"You ought to come to Lake Winston this summer. I had a wonderful time there. I won first prize in a beauty contest."
"I'd rather go to a more crowded place."

"It just shows what a name will do. Last night, I went to the theater, told them who I was, and they let me in at once without a ticket."
"Really? And who did you say you were?"

"Did you come by car?"
"Well, how do you suppose I traveled here—on my face?"
"Well, if you did, you came over an awfully rough road."

"I am studying how to become a wit in twenty lessons. I have taken ten already."
"Oh, a half a wit."

"What are you doing?"
"Shut up. I'm adding up figures in my head and every time I think of you, I add a zero."

"They say I ride as if I were part of the horse."
"Which part?"

"Porter, I'm in lower 3. Is my berth ready?"
"No, sir—I thought you politicians made up your own bunk?"

"I always throw myself into any job I undertake."
"How splendid—why don't you dig a well!"

"I thought you were dead!"
"Dead? What gave you that impression?"
"Well, I just heard someone speaking well of you!"

"I'm writing a book about the reptile family."
"I hope you'll let me read it—I just love autobiographies!"

"You'll drive me out of my mind!"
"That's no drive … that's a putt!"

"His poetry reflects his mind."
"Does it?"
"Yes. It's blank verse."

"He must have been born in a fog."
"Why?"
"Because everything he touches is missed."

The old friends had had three days together. "You have a pretty nice place here, John," said the guest on the morning of his departure. "But it looks a bit bare yet." "Oh, that's because the trees are so young," said the host, genially. "I hope they'll have grown to a good size before you come again."

"I'm the flower of my family."
"Oh, I see … a blooming idiot."

"You'd believe anything a fool told you."
"Not always … but sometimes you are quite convincing."

"It's to be a battle of wits!"
"How brave of you to go unarmed."

"What kind of man is that Jones? I don't believe I've ever met him."
"Well, if you see two men in the street and one of them looks bored to death … the other one is Jones."

"Will was just talking to you about me, wasn't he? Now, wasn't he?"
"Well, yes."
"I thought I heard him remark that I had a thick head of hair."
"Partly correct. He didn't mention your hair, however."

"That girl insulted me."
"How?"
"She asked if I danced."
"Why is that insulting?"
"I was dancing with her at the time."

"I wonder how many men will be unhappy when I marry?"
"That depends."
"On what?"
"On how many times you marry."

"Once I loved a girl and she made a fool out of me."
"What a lasting impression some girls make."

"You and he are intellectual opposites."
"What do you mean?"
"He's intellectual—and you're the opposite."

"I had a date with a mind reader last night."
"How did she enjoy the vacation?"

"Our boy was a pretty baby, but he gets more homely every day."
"Well, you didn't expect him to get to look like you all at once, did you?"

"You looked so absent-minded when I saw you this morning."
"Yes, I was wrapped up in my own thoughts."
"It's a wonder you didn't catch your death of cold."

"What happened to make your wife go on the warpath?"
"I told her that her sister looked like a baboon."
"Well, that doesn't justify her going on the warpath."
"Yes—but it's her twin sister!"

"Hey, you, waiter! Where can I wash?"
"Next corner to your right, sir. There's a sign that says 'Gentlemen Only' on the door, but don't let that stop you."

"Do you like long walks, Mr. Maxine?"
"Oh yes, mademoiselle!"
"Well, I'm not keeping you."

"Pa, what is repartee?"
"Oh, merely an insult with a dress suit on."

"I've had no luck with that girl. I've passed her every day for the last week and she hasn't smiled once."
"Yeah, some women have no sense of humor."

"I never associate with my inferiors. Do you?"
"I can't tell—I've never met your inferiors."

"I was told in my early youth that I would be feeble-minded when I grew up if I didn't stop smoking cigarettes."
"Well ... why didn't you?"

"Is your husband a bookworm?"
"No, just an ordinary one."

"I'm wrestling with my conscience."
"That ought to make a good featherweight match!"

"Lend me a nickel, I want to call up a friend."
"Here's a dime ... call up all your friends."

"What are you thinking of?"
"Nothing."
"Then take your mind off yourself."

"How long can a person live without brains?"
"Well, how old are you?"

"Are you a sculptor?"
"No. Why?"
"Well, you're a darn good chiseler."

"Do you think I can make her happy?"
"Well, she'll always have something to laugh at."

"A funny thing happened when I was born."
"You're telling me?"

"Last night I wandered in my mind."
"Well, you couldn't stray far."

"I've got a swell story to tell you. I haven't told you before."
"Is it a good story?"
"Yes, a fine one."
"Then I know you never told it to me before!"

"So he said I was a polished gentleman, did he? What were his exact words?"
"He called you a slippery fellow."

"I haven't seen you in that frock before."
"It's my twenty-first birthday present."
"Really! And now it's fashionable again?"

"I have a dreadful cold in my head."
"Well, it's better than nothing."

"Say, I have an idea!"
"Beginner's luck!"

"A lot of people have dragged his name through the mud."
"Why is that?"
"He's a tire manufacturer."

"Did you make that face at me?"
"No, sir. You just happened to walk right in front of it."

"I've changed my mind."
"Does it work any better?"

"I got an idea!"
"Treat it kind … it's in a strange place."

"They say that fish are excellent brain food. What do you suggest?"
"Why not start with a whale?"

"Define the word 'stupid.'"
"Who? Me?"
"Correct!"

"Ah, ha! I see my friend gave you a black eye."
"Why, you never saw the person that gave me this black eye."
"Nevertheless, he's my friend now."

"I asked her if I could see her home."
"And what did she say?"
"She said she would send me a picture of it."

"I'll endorse your cigarettes for no less than $100,000."
"I'll see you inhale first!"

"Why did you tell her I'm a fool?"
"Excuse me, I didn't know it was a secret."

"I used to think you were dumb when I first met you."
"Really?"
"Yes, but I wasn't sure of anything in those days."

"I have made a will leaving my brain to the hospital, and just got an acknowledgment from the authorities."
"Were they pleased?"
"They wrote that every little bit helps."

"He knows all the best people in town."
"Then why doesn't he associate with them?"
"Because they know him."

"He reminds me of a river."
"What do you mean?"
"Small at the head and big at the mouth."

"Say, do you like to play with blocks?"
"Not since I grew up."
"Then quit scratching your head."

"Do you see this chair? It's fifteenth century."
"How lovely! Did you make it yourself?"

INSURANCE

"But my dear madam, there is no insurance money for you to draw. Your late husband never insured his life; he only had a policy against fire."
"Precisely the reason I had him cremated."

"Is this a fire insurance office?"
"Yes sir, can we write you some insurance?"
"Perhaps you can. You see, my employer threatens to fire me next Saturday, and I'd like some protection."

When the agent brought Mrs. Farley her fire insurance policy, he remarked that it would be well for her to make her first payment at once. "How much will it be?" she asked. "About $100." "Oh, how tiresome!" she exclaimed. "Tell the company to let it stand and deduct it from what they owe me when the house burns down."

"Well, my dear, I've had my life insured for five thousand dollars."
"How very sensible of you! Now I don't have to keep telling you to be careful every place you go."

"I came to tell you that your policy will lapse if you do not at once pay your premium."
"Well, I'm sorry, but I've been insured in your company for eight years and nothing has happened to me yet, so I am going to try another place."

INVENTIONS

"I was in the Automat the other day and I put a lead nickel in one of those things, and what do you think came out?"
"What?"
"The manager."

"This vacuum flask will keep things hot for you indefinitely. I can very highly recommend it."
"No, thanks. I married something like that."

"Now, this instrument turns green if the liquor is good, and red if it's bad."
"Sorry, but I'm color blind. Got anything with a gong on it?"

"A professor formerly occupied this room, sir. He invented an explosive."
"Ah! I suppose those spots on the ceiling are the explosive."
"No, they're the professor."

Eve invented the walking stick when she presented Adam with a little Cain.

"Hear about the fellow who invented a device for looking through a brick wall?"
"No, what's he call it?"
"A window!"

The man that invented Life-Savers made a mint.

"My first invention was a toothless comb for baldheaded men."

A mysterious building had been erected on the outskirts of a small town. It was shrouded in mystery. All that was known about it was that it was a chemical laboratory. An old farmer, driving past the place after work had been started, and seeing a man in the doorway, called to him: "What be ye doing in this place?" "We are searching for a universal solvent—something that will dissolve all things," said the chemist. "What good will that be?" "Imagine, sir! It will dissolve all things. If we want a solution of iron, glass, gold, anything, all that we have to do is drop it in this solution." "Fine," said the farmer. "Fine … but what are ye goin' to keep it in?"

IRISH

"What are you doing there, Casey?"
"Oi'm oiling the wheelbarrow."
"Well, leave it alone. I'll do it me self. What do you know about machinery?"

"Tell me how many melons I have in the sack and I'll give you all five of them."
"Oh, I can do so; you have five."
"Take thim; but bad luck to the man that tould ye."

Two Irishmen were working on the roof of a building. One day one made a misstep and fell to the ground. The other leaned over and called, "Are you dead or alive, Mike?" "Oi'm alive," said Mike feebly. "Sure you're such a liar Oi don't know whether to belave yez or not." "Well then, Oi must be dead," said Mike, "for yez would never dare to call me a liar if Oi wor aloive."

An Irishman got a job on a skyscraper carrying mortar up to the top floor. On his first trip up he couldn't find his way down. Pat hollered to the boss, "How will I get down?" The boss yelled, "Come down the way you went up." "Faith I wunt—I come up head first!"

Clancy was chuckling. "What's the joke?" asked Mooney. "Why, Casey just bet me ten dollars he could shoot a peanut off me head with a shotgun." "What's funny about that?" "I took him up on it because I know he'll miss it!"

KISSING

"What is the mistletoe—a vine or a tree?"
"Neither—it's an excuse."

"Just one more kiss before I go."
"No, Father will be home in an hour."

"My wife only kisses me when she wants money."
"Well, isn't that often enough?"

Stealing a kiss may be petty larceny—but sometimes it's grand!

"I'm going to kiss you until the cows come home."
"Oh, but my two brothers are policemen."
"Okay, then I'll kiss you till the bulls come home."

"Stop! My lips are for another."
"Well, hold still then—and you'll get another!"

"Stop! Please don't do that! Stop! Do you hear me? Stop!"
"What do you think you're doing—writing a telegram?"

"Kisses speak the language of love."
"Well, let's talk things over."

"Now, Harry, I'm saving my kisses."
"Well, let me add one to your collection."

"Would it be wrong for me to kiss your hand?"
"Well, it would be out of place."

"Honey, your kisses are like a one-legged man."
"How's that?"
"There's a kick missing."

"Every time I kiss you it makes me a better man."
"Well, don't try to get to heaven in one night!"

"I swear I've never been kissed by any man in my life."
"Well, that's enough to make you swear."

"The only men I ever kiss are my brothers."
"What fraternity do you belong to?"

New York Girl Sells Kisses for $1 Each … pursing her lips, you might say.

KNOWLEDGE

"Your husband looks like a brilliant man. I suppose he knows practically everything."
"Don't fool yourself. He doesn't even suspect anything."

"My father and I know everything in the world."
"That so? Where is Asia?"
"That's one of the things my father knows."

"What's a miracle?"
"Do you really want to know?"
"Yes."
Whereupon the second man kicked the first in the shin.
"Did you feel that?"
"Yes!!"
"Well, if you hadn't felt that, it would have been a miracle."

LANGUAGES

"You certainly sling terrible lingo. You ought to go to London and learn the King's English."
"Oh, I know he is English."

"Did you have trouble with your French when you were in Paris?"
"No, but the Frenchmen did!"

"Betty says the French certainly are bright people. Even the children speak French."

"What's the idea of the Greens having French lessons?"
"They've adopted a French baby and want to understand what it says when it begins to talk."

"What is the Latin word for praise?"
"Laudo, sir."
"What's the matter, are you deaf?"

"Do you know that there is one word in the English language that is always pronounced wrong?"
"What word is that?"
"Wrong!"

"Why is English called the mother tongue?"
"'Cause Father never gets a chance to use it."

At roll-call in a Russian-American regiment, the officer sneezed and four soldiers answered, "Here!"

"What's Greek for boiled water?"
"Soup!"

"My brother takes up French, Spanish, Scotch, English, Swedish, Hebrew and Italian."
"Wow! Where does he study?"
"Study? He don't study—he runs an elevator."

"Can you speak French?"
Man shakes his head.
"Can you speak German?"
Man shakes his head.
"Can you speak English?"
Man shakes his head.
"It's no use, gentlemen, I've spoken to this man in three different languages and still he can't understand me!"

LATENESS

"Why are you so late?"
"A man lost a dollar bill, and there were a hundred people looking for it."
"That's no excuse."
"It certainly is. I was standing on it."

"We'll be late for the show! We've been waiting a good many minutes for that mother of mine."
"Hours, I should say."
"Ours? Oh—this is so sudden!"

"Every time I pass your house, I see you sitting by the window."
"Well, somebody has to look out for the family."

"Hello, is this the Chief of the Fire Department?"
"Yes, this is the Chief."
"Well, my house is on fire."
"How long has it been burning?"
"Half an hour."
"Did you try putting water on it?"
"Yes, but it won't go out."
"Then there ain't no use us comin' over—because that's all we could do. G'bye!"

The laziest man we know refuses even to labor under a delusion.

"Yep, he sure was lazy. I guess he was the laziest man that ever lived around these parts. When it come time for him to get married, he picked out a widow who already had three kids."

"Jack is certainly a steady boy, isn't he?"
"If he were any steadier, he wouldn't even move."

LAWYERS

"Will $25,000 for breach of promise be punishment enough for him?"
"No, I want him to marry me!"

Jones stopped beside a grave in a cemetery containing a tombstone which read: "Here lies a lawyer and an honest man." "Gosh," said Jones, "who'd ever a' thunk that that little grave could hold two men."

"If a dog steals a piece of meat from my store, is the owner liable?"
"Certainly."
"Well, your dog took a piece of meat worth about a half-dollar about five minutes ago."
"Indeed … then if you will give me the other half, that will cover my fee."

A certain rich litigant went away to his country seat at the conclusion of an important case before judgement had been pronounced. A few hours later his lawyer wired him as follows: "Right has triumphed." The rich litigant wired back: "Appeal at once."

"And how's lawyer Jones doing, doctor?"
"Poor fellow, he's lying at death's door."
"That's a lawyer for ya—at death's door and he's still lying!"

"Father, do all lawyers tell the truth?"
"Yes, my boy, lawyers will do anything to win a case."

"Why do you want a new trial?"
"On the grounds of newly discovered evidence."
"What's the nature of it?"
"My client just dug up $400 that I didn't know he had."

Lawyer: Well, if you want my honest opinion—
Client: No, no … I want your professional advice.

"The precedents are against you, madam."
"Well, sue them too."

"Did that lawyer prove you're not guilty of stealing that watch?"
"He did that."
"How did you pay him?"
"I gave him the watch."

"What are you doing on the night of June twenty-fifth?

Did you hear the one about the lawyer who spent a whole evening trying to break a girl's will?

"Are there any divorces in heaven?"
"Of course not—you can't get a divorce without a lawyer."

LAZINESS

"My mother is a very clever woman. She had the landlord's picture painted on the rug, and now father beats the rug twice a week."

The laziest woman in the world is the one who puts popcorn in her pancakes so that they'll turn over by themselves.

"How is it I scarcely ever find you fellows at work when I come in?"
"Well, sir, it's on account of those rubber heels you wear."

"Tom, I wish you wouldn't whistle at your work."
"I ain't working, boss, I'm only whistling."

"Didn't opportunity ever knock at your door?"
"Probably."
"And you didn't answer it?"
"What do you think servants are for?"

LETTERS

"What do you mean this is a postcard from your girl? There's nothing on it."
"Well, Captain, we ain't speaking."

Telegram:
DEAR HUBBY: WONDERFUL RESORT THIS STOP HAVE RUNNING WATER IN ROOM.
MARY JONES, PLEASURE LAKE MONTANA
Reply:
GET RID OF THAT DAMN INDIAN.
HUBBY

"I just got a letter from a man threatening to blow my head off if I don't stop going around with his wife."
"Well, why don't you stop going around with his wife?"
"I don't know who his wife is—he forgot to sign his name."

"What are you writing?"
"A letter to my girl."
"Why do you write so slowly?"
"Because she can't read very fast."

"Well … our son is engaged to be married. We will write and congratulate the dear boy."
"My dear boy. What glorious news! Your father and mother rejoice in your happiness. It has long been our dearest wish that you should

marry some good woman. A good woman is heaven's most precious gift to man. She brings out all the best in him and helps him to suppress all that is evil.... Your mother has gone out for a stamp ... stay single, you dope!"

"My son's letters from school always send me running to the dictionary."
"You're lucky—my son's letters always send me to the bank!"

"Why are you putting 'personal' on that letter to Mr. Jones?"
"I want his wife to open it."

Abe's boy Ikey was in the outer office when a telegram arrived, and the typist called out: "A wire from the salesman, Mr. Bernstein." "Read it aloud to me," the boss called back from the inner room. So she started, "Was in Dallas Monday stop be in Houston Wednesday stop be in New Orleans Thursday stop—" Here Abe interrupted, calling to his son: "Ikey, leave that girl alone and let her read the telegram!"

"Is there anything I can do for you?"
"Oh, it's nothing. I just got a letter from my sister. She says her husband went out shooting, and a terrible accident happened. But her handwriting is terrible ... if this is an 'o'... then he shot himself!"

Dear Jake: You're cordially invited to attend a penthouse party at Helen Morgan's house. The swellest women in town will be there with a lot of celebrities. Wine and everything. Boy, will there be a swell time. P.S. I knew you'd read so far, you dirty crook. How about the $50 you owe me?

LIES

"You ought to sleep well."
"Why?"
"You lie so easily."

"He's so crooked that the wool he pulls over your eyes is half cotton."

LOTTERIES

"Want to take a chance on an automobile? Only a dollar."
"But I don't want a car."
"That's all right, maybe you won't win it!"

"I'm putting you down for a couple of tickets for a raffle for a poor old man."
"What would I do with a poor old man?"

LOVE

"Did you tell Dot when you proposed that you weren't worthy of her?"
"Well, I was going to, but she beat me to it."

"So you asked for his daughter, did you? Well, how did you come out?"
"Through the window!"

"My boyfriend will always pause and park the car."
"Yeah, and mine always parks the car and paws!"

"How kind of you to bring me these lovely flowers. They are beautiful and fresh. I believe there is some dew on them yet."

"Boy, I'm a great lover."
"What makes you think so?"
"When I walk down the street, everyone says, 'Wow, look at that kisser!'"

"Frank's eyes make it dangerous for a girl to go driving with him. He always sees spots."
"Black spots."
"No, secluded spots."

"Since I met you I can't sleep, I can't eat, I can't drink."
"Why not?"
"I'm broke!"

"You are the sunshine of my life. Your smile falls like lightning into my soul. With you by my side I would defy all the storms of life."
"Is this a proposal or a weather report?"

"Each hour I spend with you is like a pearl to me."
"Oh, quit stringing me."

Puppy love is the beginning of a dog's life.

"If you keep looking like that, girlie, I'm going to kiss you."
"I can't keep this expression much longer!"

"I kissed Betty on the forehead last night."
"What did she do?"
"She called me down."

"Did your girl take it to heart when you broke off the engagement?"
"No, she took it to court."

"He says he thinks I am the nicest girl in town. Shall I ask him to call?"
"No, dear, let him keep on thinking so."

"I would like to marry your daughter, sir."
"Tell me, young man, do you drink?"
"Thanks! But let's settle this other thing first."

"Is he still paying as much attention to Helen as ever?"
"Not quite. They're married now."

"If I marry you, Henry, will you let me keep my job at the office?"
"Will I let you! I'm depending on it!"

"Would you marry an idiot for the sake of his money?"
"Oh, this is so sudden!"

"Why so downhearted, Bill? Wouldn't Sue wait until your rich uncle died?"
"No … she married him last night!"

"Darling, I have a confession to make. I don't know how to cook!"
"Don't worry—I'm an artist—and there won't be anything to cook!"

He was rather shy, and after she had thrown her arms around him and kissed him for bringing her a bouquet, he stood up and started to leave. "I'm sorry I offended you," she said. "I'm not offended," he said, "I'm going for more flowers!"

"Am I the first girl you ever loved?"
"No, dear, but I'm getting harder to please than I used to be."

"I wish to marry your daughter."
"Can you divorce her in the manner to which she has become accustomed?"

"I shall never marry a man whose income hasn't at least 5 noughts in it."
"Darling, mine's *all* zeroes!"

"I was nearly married once. I was all set to marry her when I suddenly changed my mind."
"What caused you to change your mind?"
"It was on account of a remark she made when I asked her to marry me."
"Well, what did she say?"
"She said no."

"I have a picture of you in my mind all the time."
"How small you make me feel!"

"You see, if we enter a compassionate marriage we can live together a while and then, if we find that we've made a mistake, we can separate."
"What will we do with the mistake?"

Usually when love flies out the window, it's a sign the husband is home again.

"Did her father come between you?"
"Worse ... behind me!"

"Sir, I've courted your daughter for fifteen years."
"Well, what do you want?"
"To marry her."
"Well, I'll be hanged. I thought you wanted a pension or something."

"Dearest, how did you recognize me? It was so dark last night."
"Oh, sweetheart, I felt it was you."

"I must study that young man of yours, daughter. I want to see how he takes hold of things that interest him."
"All right, dad, just hide behind the sofa some night."

"Are you musical?"
"No."
"Well, quit fiddling around my knee!"

"You're wealthy, aren't you, Elaine?"
"Well, I'm worth about four million.

"Will you marry me?"
"Oh, I couldn't."
"I knew it."
"Then why did you ask me?"
"I just wanted to know how a man felt when he lost four million."

"Jack seems to be stuck on Mary."
"Stuck on? You mean stuck with!"

"George proposed to me last night."
"Ah, I win my bet!"
"What bet?"
"I bet him he'd get drunk again this afternoon."

"I love you, darling. I adore you."
"Are you going to marry me?"
"Ah, don't change the subject."

"I love you, William."
"Even though I have no money?"
"I repeat—I love you like a sister!"

"I would like to marry your daughter."
"Very well, but are you able to support a family?"
"Why, er—yes."
"Very well, but you know there are ten of us?"

"Was she the kind of a girl you'd give your name to?"
"Yes, but not my right name!"

"What would you call a man who is lucky in love?"
"A bachelor."

"Heavy date you had last night. Did you have a good time?"
"Rotten."
"Why, what happened?"
"Did you ever enjoy a book with the last chapter missing?"

"Are you looking at my knee?"
"Oh stop, you know I'm above that!"

"I wonder what my boyfriend means by sending me one carnation a day, every day."
"Don't you know? He's saying it with flowers, and he stutters."

"I understand that Jim is a great ladies' man."
"Yes, he makes love to ten girls a week, approximately."
"What do you mean, approximately?"
"Roughly!"

"Jack says he can read you like a book."
"Yes, printed in Braille."

"I'm delighted to know that your father is glad I'm a poet."
"Yeah, the last boyfriend of mine he tried to throw out was a prizefighter."

"So you want to marry my daughter. Well, my answer depends on your financial position."
"What a coincidence—my financial position depends upon your answer!"

"I told her I was knee deep in love with her."
"What did she say?"
"She promised to keep me on her wading list."

"Do you love me because my father has money?"
"No, I love you for your own account."

"You used to call me the light of your life."
"But I didn't know how much it would cost me to keep it burning."

"I'm afraid your little brother saw me kiss you. What shall I give him to keep him quiet?"
"Well, he usually gets a quarter."

"Rodney proposed again last night."
"Well, are you going to marry him?"
"Oh, no—that isn't what he proposed."

"My girlfriend and I were parked on a lonely road, and a robber held us up."
"What did you lose?"
"Ten minutes!"

"Dearest, I love you and I want you for my wife."
"Heavens! I didn't know you had a wife."

"Darling, in the moonlight your teeth are like pearls."
"Oh? And when were you in the moonlight with Pearl?"

Holding hands with a man in the movies may not always indicate affection. Sometimes it's self-protection.

"Do you pet?"
"No."
"Do you drink?"
"No."
"Do you stay out late at night?"
"No."
"No bad habits at all, eh?"
"Just one."
"What's that?"
"I tell lies."

"Young man, I'll teach you to make love to my daughter!"
"I wish you would—I don't seem to be making any headway."

"And if I sit over in that nice, dark corner with you, will you promise not to hug me?"
"Yes."
"And will you promise not to kiss me?"
"Yes."
"Then why are we going over there?"

"What do you think of Dora's father?"
"That man ought to be fined for contempt of courting!"

"Dearest, do you really love me more than anyone else in the world? Do you love me enough to give me your name?"
"Sure. Willie Smith!"

"The man that marries my daughter will need lots of money."
"Well, I'm the man, then—because I need plenty!"

"Horace was over to my house last night and just as he started to leave he asked me to wear his ring, but I had to tell him I couldn't wear it until I knew him better."
"But you're wearing it now."
"Well, he didn't leave right then."

He: My treasure!
She: My treasury!

"I'm off of these college boys."
"What's wrong?"
"They start out holding your hand and pretty soon they're trying to shuffle the whole deck!"

"Anything you say goes, baby."
"Oh—Joe!"

"It doesn't matter whether I wear velvet or chiffon. You'll love me just the same, won't you?"
"I'll love you through thick and thin."

"When I talk I have to feel for my words."
"Well, they're not tattooed on me!"

"I like to take sophisticated girls home."
"I'm not sophisticated."
"Well, you're not home yet."

"Say, are you Santa Claus?"
"No. Why?"
"Then leave my stocking alone!"

"But dear, can't we live on love?"
"Sure. Your father loves you, don't he?"

"Somebody is fooling with my knee."
"It's me—and I'm not fooling!"

"If you loved a rich man and a poor man, what would you do?"
"I'd marry the rich, and be good to the poor!"

Love is like a poker game. It takes a pair to open, she gets a flush, he shows diamonds, and it ends with a full house.

"You needn't be so stuck up about finally getting engaged! I coulda married anybody I pleased!"
"Yeah, but you never pleased anybody."

"Why do they always give a shower for a girl who is going to be married?"
"It symbolizes the beginning of a reign."

"I thought you were going to marry Sally?"
"I broke my engagement with her."
"Is she taking it to heart?"
"No, she's taking it to court."

"Will you love me after we're married?"
"Of course I will, dear. I'm just crazy about married women!"

"What caused the coolness between you and that young doctor? I thought you were engaged."
"His writing is rather illegible. He sent me a note calling for 10,000 kisses. I thought it was a prescription … and I took it to the druggist to be filled."

"I don't love you."
"But when I come to your house your face always lights up."
"Oh, that's only a flash in the pan!"

"Remember the time we got caught in the revolving door?"
"Why? That wasn't the first time we met."
"No, but that was when we started going around together."

"What happened to the boy who used to bring you all those flowers?"
"He married the girl at the florist."

"Jack, are you sure it's me you're in love with, and not my clothes?"
"Test me, darling."

"Darling, will you be my wife?"
"Will you always let me do just what I like?"
"Certainly."
"Can mother live with us?"
"Of course, dear."
"Will you give up the club and always give me money when I ask for it?"
"Willingly, my pet."
"I'm sorry. I could never marry such a damn fool!"

"Only a mother could love a face like that."
"I'm about to inherit a million dollars."
"I'm about to become a mother!"

"Harry surprised me by telling me that we are going to spend our honeymoon in France."
"How nice! And how did he spring it on you?"
"He said as soon as we were married he would show me where he was wounded in the war."

"Can your girlfriend keep a secret?"
"Oh yes. We were engaged for three weeks before I even knew about it!"

"Harold took me for a ride to Connecticut last week."
"That's where you made a big mistake!"
"No, that was in Ohio."

"Dora, who sat on the newly painted bench in the garden?"
"Harold and I."
"Well, you both must have ruined your clothes."
"Only Harold."

"I've just made three wishes. The first is that you marry me."
"I'll be glad to marry you."
"That's wonderful!"
"But, what are the other two wishes?"
"I'm saving those until I see how the marriage turns out."

"Darling, I earn $2,000 a year. Do you think you can manage on that?"
"Yes, dear, but what would you live on?"

"Darling, you are everything to me."
"Ummmmmm—hold everything!"

"What do you know about love?"
"Listen. I was once in love with my third wife!"

"I am burning with love for you."
"Oh, don't make a fuel of yourself."

"Sir, may I have your daughter for my wife?"
"Bring your wife around and we'll see."

"I just committed love suicide."
"How did you do it?"
"I hung myself around my girl's neck."

LUCK

"Is it unlucky to postpone your wedding day?"
"Not if you keep on doing it."

"Do you think Friday is unlucky?
   "No, I was born on Friday."
"Well, what do your parents think?"

MARRIAGE

"Why don't you make the bread mother used to make?"
"Why don't you make the dough father used to make?"

"You say you're your wife's third husband?"
"No, I am her fourth husband."
"Heavens, man! You ain't a husband … you're a habit!"

"There goes a woman on whom I would spend my last cent."
"Would you? Well, do you know, that's my wife?"
   "Oh, is it? I'm awfully sorry."
"That's all right, she didn't hear you."

The old-fashioned wife used to darn her husband's socks, while the modern wife socks her darn husband.

"I suppose you gave the minister a fee?"
"Yes. I gave him $6."
"And what did he say?"
"Nothing. He just looked at the bride and gave me $3 back."

"You can tell she's a real lady by the way she dresses."
"I don't know. A real lady would pull down the shade."

"I'm gonna marry Jean Harlow in December."
"Did she say she would marry you in December?"
"No, but she said it would be a cold day when she marries me."

A child wakes at two o'clock in the morning and asks Mama to tell her a fairy tale. "It's too late, darling. Daddy will be in shortly and he'll tell us both one."

"There goes the city's biggest business man. Everything he touches turns to gold."
"I wonder if you could persuade him to touch this ring you bought for me."

"I've just returned from a vacation in Florida."
"Did you get much of a tan?"
"No, my husband had a man shadowing me."

"Are you secretly married to her?"
"No, she knows it."

"I'm in love with two girls."
"Well, what are you going to do about it? You can't marry them both, that would be bigamy."
"By the way, what is the penalty for bigamy?"
"Two mother-in-laws."

Before a man's married, he's a dude; after marriage, he's subdued. Before marriage he has no buttons on his shirt; after marriage he has no shirt. Before marriage he swears he would not marry the best woman in the world; after marriage he finds out that he hasn't.

"Oh, I'm so sleepy ... is everything shut up for the night?"
"That depends on you, everything else is."

Courtship is bliss, and marriage is blister.

"It says here in the paper that a certain man hasn't spoken to his wife for twelve years."
"Give him time. He may get a chance yet."

"Does the doctor think your wife is going to die?"
"Damned if I know."
"Didn't he tell you something as to the chances?"
"Yep. He told me to prepare for the worst—and damned if he hasn't got me guessing."

"Daddy, it says here that wild animals get a new set of fur each winter."
"Ssh! Don't speak so loudly, son, your mother might hear you!"

"Anybody would think I was nothing but a cook in this household."
"Not after eating a meal here!"

Before marriage a man does a lot of spooning over his sweetheart. After marriage there is less spooning and more forking over.

A thoughtful wife is one who serves the whole meal on one plate so her husband won't have too many dishes to wash.

"How long have you been married?"
"Fifteen years."
"And how old did you say your wife is?"
"Forty years old."
"How would you like to change her for two twenties?"

"When you found you couldn't accept the invitation to our wedding, why didn't you send your regrets?"
"Oh, I thought you'd have enough of your own."

"Mommy, do fairy tales always begin with 'once upon a time'?"
"No, dear. They sometimes begin, 'My love, I have been detained at the office again tonight.'"

"Congratulations, old man! Your wife has presented you with quadruplets."
"Oh—four crying out loud!"

"I have a wonderful sense of humor."
"Yes, I met your wife."

"My wife prefers tea for breakfast, while I prefer coffee."
"Then I suppose it's necessary to have both, eh?"
"Oh no, we compromise."
"In what way?"
"We have tea."

"Was she ever married before?"
"Twice."
"Why do you want to be the third?"
"Well, you know, there is nothing like dealing for an old established firm."

"You talk a great deal in your sleep."
"It's the only chance I get."

"What's a chain store?"
"A place where you buy marriage licenses."

"Darling, haven't I made you what you are?"
"Yes, and have I ever reproached you for it?"

Before marriage: he caught her in his arms. After marriage: he caught her in his pockets.

"Don't show me any more bills. I can't face them."
"I don't want you to face them, dear, I want you to foot them."

"I met your sister on the street today and she looks shorter."
"Yes, she got married and is settling down."

"He married her for her money. Wasn't that awful?"
"Did he get it?"
"No."
"That *is* awful."

"Sheep certainly are stupid animals."
"Yes, my lamb …"

"When I married you, I didn't know you were a coward. I thought you were a brave man."
"So did everybody else."

All men are born free and equal, but some get married.

"When I was engaged to my husband, he was the very light of my existence."
"And now?"
"The light goes out every night."

"Look how reluctant young men are to marry and settle down. They seem to fear marriage. Why, before I was married, I didn't know what fear was!"

"I'm a man of few words."
"I'm married, also."

"I cook and cook and what do I get for it? Nothing."
"You're lucky. I get indigestion."

"When I got married, I said I'd be boss or know the reason why."
"So you're the boss?"
"No, but I know the reason why."

"Boobleby boasts that his wife made him all that he is."
"That's not boasting, that's apologizing."

"My husband stays out until five in the morning. What would you do in my place?"
"Let's go over to your place and I'll show you."

"Does your wife miss you much?"
"No, her aim is perfect."

"They say a man isn't complete until he gets himself a wife."
"He isn't even complete then—he's finished!"

"The biggest fools always manage to marry the prettiest women."
"Are you trying to flatter me?"

"So Edith has married that young fellow that rescued her while skating? He seemed awfully shy."
"Yes, she had to break the ice."

"I remember the night you proposed to me, Henry. I just hung my head and said nothing."
"Yes, and that's the last time I ever saw you that way."

"Where did you get that hat? It doesn't even fit you."
"It's a surprise present from my wife."
"A surprise?"
"Yeah, last night I came home unexpectedly and I found this hat on the table."

"Before we were married, you used to say that you could listen to my sweet voice all night."
"Yes, but at that time I had no idea I'd ever have to do it!"

"I want to do some shopping today, dear, if the weather is favorable. What does the paper say?"
"Rain, hail, thunder and lightning."

"Why did you tell the neighbors that you married me because I was such a good cook when you know I can't even boil a potato?"
"I had to make *some* excuse, my dear."

"I am forced to admit that women are inferior to men."
"What makes you say that?"
"My wife."

"I'm afraid the mountain climate would disagree with me."
"It wouldn't dare."

"I've just given my wife a fur coat."
"To keep her warm?"
"No, to keep her quiet."

"What is your favorite dish, Mrs. O'Rouke?"
"The heaviest one I can lay me hands on."

"I didn't like that new secretary of yours, so I discharged her this morning."
"Before giving her a chance?"
"No, before giving *you* a chance."

"Henry, I see that in Sumatra a wife can be bought for twenty-five cents. Isn't that awful?"
"I suppose prices are just high there."

How is a bride to know who is the best man at her wedding when only her husband goes on the honeymoon?

"I'm sure I don't know where little Johnny gets all his faults from. I'm sure it's not from me."
"No, you're right, dear. You haven't lost any of yours."

"Gee, I'm big-hearted."
"Why so?"
"I married two girls. Wasn't that bigamy?"

"My husband has very few faults; he doesn't gamble and he doesn't drink."
"Does he smoke?"
"Well, after a good dinner at home, he may light a cigar, but that's no more than perhaps once in six months."

"Have you heard that Brown's daughter is getting married?"
"Who's the happy man?"
"Brown."

"Before you married me, you told me you were well off."
"I was, but I didn't know it!"

"Did you know that this beautiful silk dress came from a poor little insignificant worm?"
"Yes. I'm that worm."

"You buried your wife just six months ago. If she knew how you were tearing around, she'd dig out of her grave."
"Let her dig. I buried her face down."

"Your Honor, he broke every dish in the house over my head and treated me cruelly."
"Did your husband apologize for what he had done?"
"No, Your Honor, you see, the ambulance took him away before he could talk to me."

Evolution of a letter:

My Dear Miss Smith:
Dear Miss Smith:
Dear Mary:
Mary Dear:
Dearest Mary:
Mary Darling:
Mary, beloved:
My Soulmate:
Darling Wife:
Dear Mary:
Hello Mame:
Pay to the order of Mrs. Mary S. Jones:

"What's the best month to get married in?"
"Octembruary."
"Why, there's no such month."
"You're telling me?"

In the ideal marriage the wife is a treasure and the husband is a treasury.

"I say, old man, what happened to that parrot of yours?"
"Oh, I married, you know, and it died of a broken heart. Well, not exactly. It couldn't stand the competition."

"Pa, a woman's a man's better half, isn't she?"
"We are told so, my son."
"Then, if a man marries twice, there isn't anything left of him, is there?"

"Why haven't you mended these holes in my socks?"
"Did you buy the coat you promised me?"
"No-no."
"Well, if you don't give a wrap, I don't give a darn."

Wife: Are all men fools?
Hubby: No, dear. Some are single.

"How much do I have to pay for a marriage license?"
"Two dollars down and your entire salary each week for the rest of your life."

The curate of a large and fashionable church was endeavoring to teach the significance of white to a Sunday school class. "Why does a bride invariably desire to be clothed in white at her marriage?" As no one answered, he explained, "White stands for joy, and the wedding day is the most joyous occasion of a woman's life."
A small boy queried, "Then why do all the men wear black?"

"Why does a woman take the name of the man she marries?"
"Well, she takes everything else, so she might as well take that too."

"Wilt thou take this woman to be thy lawfully wedded wife?" "I wilt."

If you want your wife to miss you—duck!

"Darling, the new maid has burned the bacon and eggs. Would you be satisfied with a couple of kisses for breakfast?"
"Sure, bring her in."

"I'm having trouble supporting my wife."
"You don't know what trouble is. Try not supporting her."

She: You're becoming unbearable! It will soon be impossible to live with you!
He: How soon?!!

Some months after the elopement, an old friend met the bridegroom and asked him eagerly for details: "What about her father? Did he catch you?"
"And how! The old man is still living with us!"

Jean: So you married your employer. How long did you work for him?
Jane: Until I got him.

Wife: (On returning from a party) Do you realize what you did?
Husband: No, but I'll admit it was wrong. What was it?

"I wanted to get married at twenty but father said I didn't have sense enough, so I waited until I was thirty."
"And you married at thirty?"
"No, I had too much sense then."

"Do you act toward your wife as you did before you married her?"
"Exactly. I remember how I used to act when I first fell in love with her. I used to lean over the fence in front of her house and gaze at her shadow on the curtain, afraid to go in. And I act just the same way now."

"Who gave you the black eye?"
"A bridegroom for kissing his wife after the ceremony."
"But surely he didn't object to that ancient custom."
"No, but it was two years after the ceremony."

"My wife explored my pockets again last night."
"What did she get?"
"About the same as any other explorer—enough material for a lecture."

"What cured him of arguing with his wife?"
"Arguing with his wife."

"My wife's lipstick seems to have a different taste from other women's."
"Yes, sort of orange flavor, isn't it?

"When you proposed to her I'll bet she said, 'This is so sudden!'?"
"No, she said, 'The suspense was terrible.'"

"Your husband seems to be a man of rare gifts."
"He is. He hasn't given me one since we were married."

"I've half a mind to get married."
"That's all you need!"

"Do you know it's possible for a wife to telephone her husband on the opposite side of the earth?"
"Then what's the use of going to the opposite side?"

Modern marriage is just like a cafeteria: a man grabs what looks nice to him and pays for it later.

MEDICINE

"Why are you skipping rope?"
"I took my medicine and forgot to shake the bottle."

MEMORY

"My wife has the worst memory I ever heard of."
"Forgets everything, eh?"
"No, remembers everything."

"What's that piece of cord tied around your finger for?"
"My wife put it there to remind me to post her letter."
"And did you do it?"
"No, she forgot to give it to me."

"I've been trying to think of a word for weeks and weeks."
"Won't 'months' do?"

Amnesia Victim: I can't remember who I am or where I live, but here's my wife's photograph.
Cop: You're a lucky man.

"I saw the doctor today about my loss of memory."
"What did he do?"
"He made me pay in advance."

MONEY

"I save a hundred dollars every day."
"You save a hundred dollars every day! How do you do it?"
"I ride to work on the subway every morning where there is a hundred-dollar fine for spitting ... and I don't spit."

If a man owns a big automobile, it doesn't prove that he has money. It only proves that he had money.

"As soon as I wear out my shoes I'll pay you."
"What has your shoes got to do with paying me back?"
"When my shoes wear out, I'll be on my feet again."

"You see that girl? She got $200,000 for a short love story."
"That's a lot of dough for a short story. What producer did she sell the picture rights to?"
"Producer, hell! She sold it to a jury."

"When you arranged for the credit, you said you and your partner had $100,000 between you. Was that statement true?"
"Sure, it was true. I lived on one side of the bank and he lived on the other."

"American Steel broke 102 today."
"I know. My old man was one of them!"

"I just bought some Mae West stock."
"What do you mean?"
"Maybe it'll come up sometime."

"I heard that when Mrs. Smythe died she left seventy thousand dollars in her bustle."
"Boy, that's a lot of money to leave behind."

"Didn't I say my ship would come in this week?"
"Were you right?"
"Sure ... my salary was docked."

"Did you ever see a three-dollar bill?"
"No."
"Here's one from my dentist."

"I understand your brother is very wealthy."
"Oh yes, he became wealthy through a sudden upward movement of oil."
"What oil stock did he buy?"
"He didn't buy any. A rich old aunt tried to start a fire with a can of it."

"It is reported that eggs are used in Armenia as currency."
"It must be a messy job getting cigarettes out of a machine."

"It's great to be famous. Just think of all the prominent men who die and have their faces on a ten-dollar bill."
"That's nothing. I'd rather be alive and have my hands on one."

"What's the best check protector?"
"A fountain pen that won't write."

[Used in the film *Spider-man 2*]
"Have any of you dropped a roll of bills with an elastic band around them?"
"Yes, I have!" cried a dozen voices.
"Well, I found the elastic."

There was a Jew on the train. He was trying to get up a game of poker. He asked the Irishman if he wanted to play. The Irishman said, "No. For three reasons. First—I have no money." The Jew said, "The hell with the other two!"

"Have you heard that Jones the millionaire died?"
"Yes, and I'm terribly sorry."
"Why, he was no relation of yours, was he?"
"No, that's why I'm sorry."

Girl's father: My daughter tells me you are worth over ten thousand dollars.
Suitor: That's right. Expectation of life—35 years. Salary—300. 35 times 30—well, you can work it out for yourself.

"I just burned up a $100 bill."
"You must be a millionaire."
"Well, it's easier to burn them than to pay them."

MOTHERS-IN-LAW

"And when we're married, darling, we'll have a nice little house right near mother so she can drop in anytime."
"You bet. We'll get one right by the river."

"I don't like my mother-in-law."
"Listen, don't you realize that you wouldn't have your wife if it wasn't for your mother-in-law?"
"Yes, that's why I don't like her!"

"My mother won't stay in this house another minute if we don't get rid of the mice. Say, where are you going?"
"Out to drown the cat!"

"You are charged with throwing your mother-in-law out of the window."
"I done it without thinking, sir."
"Yes, but don't you see how dangerous it would have been to anyone passing at that time."

"I just saw a man stand by while his mother-in-law was being slandered."
"I'd do the same thing."
"What! Do you mean to say you'd stand by and see your mother-in-law get slandered?"
"Oh, I beg your pardon! I thought you said slaughtered."

"I hear your mother-in-law died recently."
"Yes, she did."
"Well, it's hard to lose a mother-in-law."
"Hard! Why, it's almost impossible!"

MUSIC

Comedy Song Titles:
1. She Knocked My Apartment So I Knocked Her Flat
2. She Broke My Heart So I Broke Her Jaw
3. We Feed the Children Garlic So We Can Find Them in the Dark
4. Take Back Your Heart, I Ordered Liver

"I'm sorry you don't think much of my voice, Professor. The people next door say I ought to go abroad to study."
"Yes, but I don't live next door."

"I play the piano just to kill time."
"You certainly have a fine weapon."

"I had to give up my musical career."
"Why?"
"The money died."

"Does my practicing on the sax annoy you?"
"It did when I first heard the neighbors discussing it, but I'm getting so that I don't care what happens to you."

I was playing "My Old Kentucky Home" when a man began to cry. I said to him, "Are you a Kentuckian, sir?" He answered, "No, I'm a musician."

"What key are playing in?"
"Skeleton key."
"Skeleton key?"
"Yeah, it fits anything."

"By the way, old chap, when at school you used to be rather fond of music. Do you play any instrument now?"
"Yes. Second fiddle at home."

"Do you play an instrument?"
"Yes, I'm a cornetist."
"And your sister?"
"She's a pianist."
"Does your mother play?"
"She's a zitherist."
"And your father?"
"He's a pessimist."

"How is the music in the restaurant?"
"Wonderful! I was in there with my wife the other evening and couldn't hear a word she said!"

"You want us to play at the funeral? Is it a military funeral?"
"No, it is the funeral of my brother. He was a private citizen. He requested that your band should play at his funeral."
"My band? Why should he choose my band?"
"He said he wanted everybody to feel sorry he died."

"Why doesn't your wife sing to the baby when it cries?"
"Sh! We've found out that the neighbors would rather listen to the baby."

"They tell me you love good music."
"Oh, that doesn't matter. Please go on."

"I play violin by ear."
"That's nothing. My uncle fiddles with his whiskers."

The grumpy old man was compelled to sit right next to the orchestra in the restaurant. When the selection came to an end, he called the leader and said, "Would you be so kind as to play something by request?"
"Certainly, anything you like, sir."
"Then, please be good enough to play a game of checkers until I finish my meal."

"My brother is a champion long-distance cornet player. He entered a contest once and played 'Annie Laurie' for three weeks."
"Did he win?"
"No, the other fellow played 'Stars and Stripes Forever.'"

"My daughter has arranged a little piece for the piano."
"Good! It's about time we had a little peace."

"At the Union Church next Sabbath morning there will be special music by the choir, assisted by the new organist. The church will be closed the following three Sundays for repair."

"I don't know why but this song I am playing seems to haunt me."
"Naturally. You murdered it."

"I'm going to give you this violin."
"An out-and-out gift?"
"Absolutely. No strings attached."

NAMES

"Well, I got bolder and I asked her her name, which she said was Helen French. Then I said, 'What is it in German?'"

"Maud is only twenty-five, but she's married three times. And all her husbands have been named William."
"I see. She was a Bill collector."

"Let's go call on The Tonsil Sisters."
"Why do they call them The Tonsil Sisters?"
"Because nearly everybody has had them out."

The efficient lady guide was showing the visitor around the reservation. "Over there is Rain-in-the-Face. They call her that because she's always crying. Next to her is a girl whose name, when translated into English, is Flower-with-the-ears-that-flap-in-the-wind. You see, all those who live here have names which indicate some noticeable physical characteristic. Simple, isn't it?"
"I'll say it is, Fanny."

Two men and a woman were on a train headed for California and decided they had better get acquainted.
One man said, "My name is Paul, but I'm not an apostle."
The other said, "My name is Peter, but I'm not a saint."
The girl said, "My name is Mary, and I don't know what to say!"

A: What's your name?
B: Quitz Jones.
A: Where did you get the name 'Quitz'?
B: When I was born my father came in and saw me and said to my mother, "Mary, let's call it Quitz."

One day a woman by the name of Helen Hunt found a pocketbook with about a hundred dollars in it. Being a loyal churchgoer she decided to give it to her minister and let him try and find the owner. The good man made the announcement this way: "I am requested to announce that a pocketbook has been found. If anyone present has lost one, he is requested to go to Helen Hunt for it."

A: Why do you call your sweetheart 'Pilgrim'?
B: Because every time he comes he makes more progress.

"What's your name?"
"Minnehaha!"
"What's so funny about that?"

"Why do you call the baby 'Bill?'"
"He was born on the first of the month."

"Why do you call your girl 'Appendix'?"
"Because everyone has had her out."

A witness, in describing certain events, said, "The person I saw at the head of the stairs was a man with one eye named Jacob Wilkins."
"What was the name of his other eye?" asked the lawyer.

NEIGHBORS

"We are going to be living in a better neighborhood soon."
"So are we."
"What? Are you moving, too?"
"No, we're staying here."

"There's one good thing about having a Scotch family for neighbors. Take that family upstairs. Like all upstairs families, they like to give parties. But they never keep us awake with their dancing. When we want them to stop dancing, we merely turn off our radio."

"What is your nationality, sir?"
"I'm a Highball, sir."
"A Highball?"
"Yes, half Scotch and half Celt, sir."

"I'm a neighbor of yours now. I live right across the river."
"Indeed! I hope you drop in some day."

NEWLYWEDS

"You never take the slightest interest in anything I do," sobbed the young bride.
"Now don't be unreasonable, darling," said the groom. "All last night I lay awake wondering what you had put in that cake you made yesterday!"

The bride was very much concerned at seeing twin beds in the bridal suite.
"What's the matter, dearest?" asked the groom.
"Why," she replied, "I certainly thought we were going to get a room all to ourselves!"

Bride: I want a pound of mince meat and—and—
Butcher: Yes?
Bride: And would you mind telling me what kind of an animal the mince is?

The waiter came over to the newlyweds to take their order for dinner.
"Some honeymoon salad," said the groom.
"Honeymoon salad?" asked the waiter. "What is that?"
"Just lettuce alone!" replied the groom.

NEWSPAPERS

"I sent some suggestions for the improvement of your paper. Have you carried out any of my ideas?"
"See that office boy with the wastebasket?"
"Yes."
"Well, he's carrying out your ideas."

Editor: Well, what did our eminent statesman have to say?
Reporter: Nothing.
Editor: Well, keep it down to a column.

"Hello, is that the editor? This is George W. Boggs. I want to talk about that notice of my death in your newspaper yesterday."
"Yes, Mr. Boggs—where are you speaking from, please?"

"I thought your paper was friendly to me."
"So it is. What's the matter?"
"I made a speech at the dinner last night and you didn't print a line of it."
"Well, what further proof do you want?"

"What should I say about the two peroxide blondes who made such a fuss at the game?"
"Why, just say the bleachers went wild."

The proprietor of a certain newspaper walks five miles each morning to keep up his circulation.

"I've got a perfect news story!"
"The man who bit the dog?"
"No, the bull who threw the congressman!"

NIGHTCLUBS

He who dances must pay the piper—also the headwaiter, the waiter, the flower girl, the hatcheck boy, the doorman and the cab driver!

Café Owner: No more tables, sir, we're filled up.
Man: But there's space for another table there.
Café Owner: Sorry, sir, that's the dance floor.

"How did you find yourself this morning after the party?"
"I just looked under the table and there I was!"

OBESITY

Fat man: Joseph, did you get me two seats on the train so I could be comfortable?
Butler: Yes, sir. One in the sleeper and one in the parlor car.

"Your brother's wife must weigh about three hundred pounds, doesn't she?"
"She is quite stout, but he thinks a lot of her."
"Well, he sure has a lot to think about!"

"Young man, can I get into the park through this gate?"
"Guess so, lady—I just saw a load of hay go through."

Never laugh at a fat woman—she's just a little girl gone to waist!

"I lost twenty pounds when I was in England."
"How much is that in American money?"

"Stop pushin', willya?"
"I ain't pushin' … I only sighed."

She's so fat that she has to walk upstairs backward, to keep from stepping on herself.

"Oh, well," sighed the stylish stout woman as she heard a loud snap in the vicinity of her reducing girdle, "they said it would reduce the hips or bust."

There's a woman who was so fat that she rocked herself to sleep trying to get up.

"A friend of mine had a boy that was very thin. But he made him fat in ten seconds."
"You astonish me."
"It's a fact. He threw the boy out of the window and he came down plump."

"She was fat, but she could dance like a fairy. That is, a fairy her size."

"She was so thin that she had to eat spaghetti one at a time."

OFFICE

"The boss discharged the three prettiest stenographers we had."
"Canning peaches at this time of year ..."

"So, you would like to be my typist?"
"Yes, sir."
"What are your qualifications?"
"I know your wife by the sound of her footsteps."

"I had to let my stenographer go because she wasn't experienced."
"What was the trouble?"
"She didn't know anything except shorthand and typing."

"Was that pretty typist fired?"
"No, she quit because she caught the boss kissing his wife."

"How many stenographers have you?"
"Two."
"I've only seen one."
"I've got a worse looking one to show my wife."

"There's a salesman outside with a mustache."
"Tell him I have a mustache."

"How many people work in your office?"
"About half."

OLD AGE

"My grandfather lived to ninety-seven years and never used glasses."
"Remarkable!"
"Yeah, he always drank out of the bottle."

"107! How did he manage to live to be 107?"
"Well, you see, he didn't smoke, drink, swear and he always stayed out in the fresh air."
"Why, I had an uncle who did all those things, but he died at 57 years of age."
"Well, you see, he didn't do them things long enough."

"Doctor, I want to live to be a hundred years old. How can I do it?"
"Do you drink?"
"No."
"Do you smoke?"
"No."
"Do you chase women?"
"No."
"Then what do you want to be a hundred years old for?"

OLD MAIDS

Two spinsters were discussing men:
"Which would you desire most in your husband—brains, wealth, health or appearance?"
"Appearance, and the sooner the better!"

"Porter."
"Yes, madam, what is it you wish?"
"I just found two strange men in my apartment and I want you to put one of them out."

OPTIMISTS

An optimist is a guy who thinks his wife has quit smoking cigarettes when he finds cigar butts around the house.
A pessimist is a man who has lived with an optimist.

PAWNSHOP

"My brother has a medal for running five miles, and one for ten miles; a silver medal for swimming; two cups for wrestling, and badges for boxing and rowing."
"He must be a wonderful athlete."
"He's no athlete at all. He owns a pawnshop."

PERSONAL APPEARANCE

"She's so cross-eyed that when she cries, the tears roll down her back."
"Really?"
"Yes, the doctor is treating her for bacteria."

"He says that it's glasses that make his nose so red."
"Glasses of what?"

Dear Editor: Can a girl do anything about an unattractive knee?
Answer: Sure! Grin and bear it.

She had Western teeth—the kind with wide-open spaces.

"George's moustache makes me laugh."
"It tickles me, too."

"I inherit my features from my father."
"It's just too bad he didn't make a will and cut you off!"

"That Russian you introduced me to last night has sparrow eyes."
"You mean they are brown?"
"No, they flit from limb to limb."

"I think Marie's face is like a beautiful poem."
"Well, it certainly has plenty of good lines in it."

"Why do you comb your hair straight back?"
"I'm using a comb that's an heirloom and I don't want to part with it."

"I paid my fourth visit to the beauty shop today."
"Strange you can't seem to get waited on, dear."

"Where did you get that beautiful black eye?"
"You know that waitress at the Greasy Spoon whose husband is in Chicago?"
"Yeah."
"Well, he isn't."

"You know, a man can't choose his face, nor his hair, nor his eyes. He's lucky if he can pick his teeth."

"Do you think that my mustache is becoming?"
"It may be coming but it hasn't arrived yet."

"You dirty boy! Why don't you wash your face? I can see what you had for breakfast this morning."
"What was it?"
"Eggs."
"Wrong—that was yesterday!"

"My, you look beautiful tonight."
"Yes—I took a beauty nap this afternoon and overslept!"

PESTS

"The evening wore on," continued the man who was telling the story.
"Excuse me," interrupted the would-be wit, "but can you tell us what the evening wore on that occasion?"
"I do not know that it is important," replied the storyteller, "but if you must know, it was the close of a summer day."

PHOTOGRAPHERS

"$25 for a photograph! That's a terrible price."
"Well, I can do it for $15, but I'm afraid people will recognize you in a $15 picture."

"The picture would look much better if your wife had put her hand on your shoulder."
"It'd be more natural looking if she had put her hand in my pocket."

"I don't like these pictures. They don't do me justice."
"Justice? Lady, what you want is mercy."

"You say this is a photograph of your husband outside Old Kid McCoy's saloon? I see the saloon all right, but I don't see your husband."
"My Gawd, has he gone in there again?"

POLICEMEN

One day many years ago the telephone in the office of the chief of police rang.
"A man has been robbed down here on my Union Avenue beat, and I've got one of them!"
"Which one have you got?"
"The man that was robbed!"

"If you were ordered to disperse a crowd, what would you do?"
"I'd pass around the hat."

POLITENESS

"You took your hat off to that lady. Do you know her?"
"No, but I'm wearing my brother's hat, and he knows her."

"A very polite sneak thief came into our house yesterday."
"Polite?"
"Yes. He lifted all the hats he found in the hallway."

POLITICS

The secret of being a good politician is never to open your mouth unless you have nothing to say.

"The people won't elect me because of my youth."
"But you are fifty and your youth is spent."
"That's the trouble—they found out how I spent it."

"There's a fellow who has chased around for years trying to land a political job."
"What does he do now?"
"Nothing. He got the job."

"What do you think of the candidates?"
"Well, the more I think of them, the more pleased I am that only one of them can get in."

Politician (boarding train): Is my berth ready?
Porter: Nah. I thought you politicians always made up your own bunk.

"What's Bill in jail for now?"
"Political Taxidermy."
"What?"
"You heard me—he was caught stuffing ballot boxes."

A skull half an inch thick, and unearthed in Arizona, has been sent to Washington without the formality of an election.

PREACHERS

A golfing minister had been beaten badly on the links by a parishioner thirty years his senior, and had returned to the clubhouse rather disgruntled.
"Cheer up," his opponent said. "Remember, you win at the finish. You'll probably be burying me some day."
"Even then," said the preacher, "it will be your hole!"

One Sunday morning a new pastor in his first charge, announced nervously, "I will take for my text the words, 'And they fed five men with five thousand loaves of bread and two thousand fishes."
At this misquotation, an old parishioner from his seat said audibly, "That's no miracle—I could do it myself."
The young preacher said nothing at the time, but the next Sunday he announced the same text again. This time he got it right. "And they fed five thousand men on five loaves of bread and two fishes."
He waited a moment, then looking at the same man, asked, "And could you do that, too, Mr. Smith?"

"Of course I could," Mr. Smith replied.
"And how would you do it?" asked the preacher.
"With what was left over from last Sunday!"

PRISON

"$30 or thirty days. Which do you want?"
"Give me the thirty bucks, Judge. I need a new suit."

"What are you doing in here, my good man?"
"Well, I want to be a warden—so I thought I would start at the bottom."

"Jones was a model prisoner, respected by the warden and all his fellow prisoners."
"I see. 'For he's a jolly good felon!'"

"Have you anything to offer the court before sentence is passed upon you?"
"No, Your Honor. My lawyer took my last ten bucks."

A murderer was about to meet his doom. The warden asked him, "Is there one last favor I can do for you?"
"Yeah, you can hold my hand while I'm sittin' in the chair."

"Remember—anything you say will be held against you."
"Greta Garbo!"

"It is our custom to let the prisoners work at their former occupations."
"That will suit me fine, warden. I'm a traveling salesman."

"Put me in cell 39."
"What for?"
"It's the one Father used to have."

"You have a kind face. What are you in for?"
"I got twenty years for robbing my kid brother."
"Twenty years for that?"
"He was cashier at the First National."

PROBLEMS

"Here's a problem for you, old man. A donkey was tied to a rope six feet long. 18 feet away there was a bundle of hay, and the donkey wanted to get to the hay. How did he manage it?"
"Oh, I've heard that one before. You want me to say, 'I give up' and you'll say, 'So did the other donkey.'"
"Not at all."
"Then how did he do it?"
"Just walked up to the hay and ate it."
"But you said he was tied to a rope six feet long."
"So he was. But you see, the rope wasn't tied to anything. Quite simple, isn't it?"

"What was the problem?"
"Fourteen from sixteen. What's the difference?"
"What's the difference? I don't care, either."

"Tommy, what is one third of three seventeeths?"
"I don't know, but it's not enough to worry about."

PUNS

Alp - a cry of distress
Ankle - father's brother
Antic - old, ancient
Apostrophe - a terrible happening, a great calamity
Argue - a kind of a fever
Artery - where an artist works
Aspirant - taken to relieve headaches
Atom - the first man on earth
Auditor - the guy what says whether this'll be printed or not
Ballast - to blow to pieces
Bribe - a girl about to be married
Cabbage - a small taxi
Campaign - a sort of bubbly wine
Carp - slang for policeman
Cataract - the name of a high-priced car
Cattle - a household utensil used for making tea

Contest - female Count
Curtail - the appendage at the hindmost part of a dog
Dogma - a female canine with pups
Doze - the quantity of medicine to be taken at one time
Eloquent - big animal with a trunk
Feline - a guy who is sent up the river
Feudal - useless, ineffectual
Florist - a carpenter's assistant who puts in floors
Foreground - a golf course
Foundry - the receiving end of a lost-and-found department
Fuzzy - inclined to grumble
Geezer - a water phenomena of Yellowstone National Park
Gender - caretaker of the building
Goblet - a small sailor
Graph - a long-necked animal
Grovel - used in the making of roads
Grudge - a place where you keep your car
Guess - a lighter-than-air material used to fill balloons
Halter - an armed sentry
Humbug - a type of insect
Indemnify - to recognize
Idiom - person of low intelligence
Insulate - to pass a bad remark
Judicious - Hebrew chinaware
Mention - dwelling place of the idle rich
Monogram - a one-word telegram
Moron - the early part of the day
Otter - to give voice to your thoughts
Pack - a fourth of a bushel
Paunch - to beat or strike
Pauper - a male parent
Pause - father's
Pennants - what we eat at the circus
Pension - squeezing or nipping
Pepper - a printed news journal
Phase - the anterior portion of the head
Pigeon - the act of tossing something
Pillow - a great wave of the sea
Pinnacle - a card game

Pitch - a fruit known for its fuzzy skin
Plush - a reddening of the face from modesty
Pomp - a mechanical device above a well
Pot - having little or no income
Poultry - a form of literature in rhyme
Prattle - something the baby plays with
Pucker - a card game where the players bet on hands
Rack - to cause the destruction of
Radish - the color of brick
Robber - an elastic material used for garters
Rogue - something on the floor
Scandal - a sort of slipper
Scrutiny - when a lot of sailors go on strike
Shoulder - man in the army
Slipper - captain of a ship
Tactics - the sound a clock makes
Tuna - piano adjuster
Unaware - what you wear beneath your pants
Vacuum - where the Pope resides
Vice versa - dirty songs set to Italian music
View - not very many
Viper - something used to clean the pen with
Voluble - precious; gold is a voluble metal
Voter - what you drink when there's nothing better around
Wan - the first number in the Arabic system
Wicked - that which burns in a lamp
Willow - lady whose husband is dead
Wit - a grain, most important in cereal
Wrist - played by those who can't play bridge
Zoo - to institute legal proceedings against

"Ed Jones is gonna name the new arrival Ed. He figures two Eds are better than one."

"His father made his money selling soup."
"Ah—a bouillonaire!"

"Use a sentence with the words conscience stricken."
"Don't conscience strickens before they're hatched."

"They had to put him in a private cell because he was too crazy for wards."

"What's the richest country in the world?"
"Ireland."
"Ireland? What's your proof?"
"Well, her capital has been Dublin for years."

"Give me a sentence using the word 'miniature.'"
"The miniature asleep you begin to snore."

"That's a strange clock you have in the hall."
"Yes, we call it the Guest."
"Why?"
"It won't go!"

They call her Miss Atlantic City because she has a bored walk.

"Let me have a sentence with the word 'archaic' in it."
"We can't have archaic and eat it, too."

"Gimme a sentence with the word 'adamant' in it."
"Adamant Eve was the foist people in the woild."

Doctor: Have you any scars on you?
Patient: No, but I can give you a cigarette.

"Have you heard the story about the nasty military officer?"
"No, what about him?"
"He was rotten to the corps."

"It's raining cats and dogs outside."
"I know, I just stepped in a poodle."

"There's a guy who wanted his son to be a carpenter, so he sent him to a boarding school."

"What's the difference between a phrenologist, one who reads the bumps on your head, and a man who runs into a door in the dark?"
"I don't know."
"One knows de bumps, and de other bumps de nose."

Eve: Adam, dear, close your eyes so I can come home.
Adam: What's the matter?
Eve: I'm A.W.O.L.!

A frat dance is one of those affairs at which you come in like a lion and go out like a lamp.

When an Arab of the desert wants to inquire if his sister is going away from home for a while, he says, "Are you going oasis?"

A patrol wagon may not be much of a car, but it'll do in a pinch.

"What's the difference between a snake and a piano?"
"Well, you write both with a 'b.'"
"What—snake and piano?"
"No—'both'!"

"Old Bimbo is too darned fond of gold diggers. Why, he's paying the rent on a dozen apartments right now."
"Well, he believes in suites to the sweet."

"I cancelled my trip to Europe."
"Well—non-voyage!"

"How did you get so many calluses?"
"Calisthenics."

"Tough luck," said the egg in the monastery. "Out of the frying pan into the friar."

Farmer: But how can I get you to that bridge game in town if the snow is over the car's fenders?
Wifey: My dear, you simply sleigh me!

Professor: Time is money? How can you prove that time is money?
Student: Well, if you give twenty-five cents to a couple of tramps, that's a quarter to two.

"Oh dear! I can't find a pin anywhere. I wonder where all the pins go to anyway."
"That's a difficult question to answer. Because they are always pointed in one direction and headed in another."

Would you say that a girl who is out of breath is in short pants?

"What would a nation be without women?"
"A stagnation, I guess."

"What is it that's bought and still don't go to the buyer?"
"Coal, because it goes to the cellar."

"He has two wooden legs. How can he walk?"
"I guess he just lumbers along."

"I'm certainly worried about him. All he eats lately is doughnuts. He's getting to be a terrible dunkard."

"It looks like rain."
"What does?"
"Water."

"Why, I can't marry you. You're practically penniless."
"That's nothing. The Czar of Russia was Nicolas!"

"I came near selling my shoes today."
"How's that?"
"Well, I had 'em half soled."

"I play poker with potato chips."
"What kind of poker is that?"
"Spud poker."

"What state is Capa City in?"
"Never heard of it."
"Look. It's listed on this coal car—Capacity 87,000."

"What day does the sausage come out to look at its shadow?"
"You don't mean sausage. You mean ground hog."
"Well, ain't a sausage a ground hog?"

"Use despair in a sentence."
"We had a flat tire today and papa had to use despair."

"I've just been radioed."
"Radioed?"
"My girl turned me down, gave me the air."
"What's that got to do with radio?"
"I was broad-casted!"

"I can stay awake any length of time simply by forcing myself."
"I see. The triumph of mind over mattress."

"That man's a street cleaner."
"How do you know?"
"I can tell by his guttural accent."

"They say there's alcohol in bread."
"Yeah? Well, let's drink a little toast!"

"What are the children of the Czar called?"
"Czardines."

A stoic is a bird that brings babies, and a cynic is where they wash them.

"Yes, children, the Indian's wife is called a squaw. Now, what are the Indian babies called?"
"Squawkers."

"So you went for a walk with that landscape gardener? How was he?"
"Oh, a little rough around the hedges."

"How did Charlie and Mary get acquainted with each other?"
"They sang in the same church choir."
"Oh, I see, they met by chants."

"You say he married her for her money?"
"Yeah, it was a case of loaf at first sight."

"Pa, Willie's jabbing me in the eye with his joke book."
"Willie, don't poke fun at your brother!"

"What did you do last night?"
"Well, I often wondered where the sun went at night—so I stayed up and it finally dawned on me!"

"Why did your boss fire you from your last job?"
"Sinus trouble."
"You mean to tell me that your boss fired you because you had sinus trouble?"
"Yeah—I sinus name to a bad check!"

"You know, I went to an immoral school before I came here."
"Immoral?"
"Yeah—we didn't have any principal."

"If a man smashed a clock, could he be accused of killing time?"
"Not if he could prove that the clock struck first."

QUIPS

"What did Juliet say to Romeo when she saw him in the balcony?"
"Why the hell didn't you get seats in the orchestra?"

"Well, the days sure are getting longer."
"Why, Jimmie—when did you get married?"

"Sire, would you give five dollars to bury a saxophone player?"
"Here's thirty dollars. Bury six of them!"

"According to statistics, someone dies every time I breathe."
"How about using mouthwash?"

"Your broker is calling for more margin and the laundryman wants his money. Which one shall I pay?"
"It don't make any different. I'll lose my shirt either way."

"Listen, do you know how to bring up a child?"
"Of course I do."
"Well, you've better hurry, your kid just fell in the well."

"Can you tell me how I can find the chemistry building?"
"Sure, ask somebody."

"Do you file your fingernails?"
"No. After I cut them, I throw them away."

"Do you think it will stop raining?"
"It always has."

"Why do you call your dog Crystal?"
"Because he's a watchdog."

"Why do you use such a long cigar holder?"
"My doctor told me to keep away from tobacco."

"What's the difference between mashed potatoes and pea soup?"
"Well, anybody can mash potatoes!"

"How in the world did Ruth break into the movies? I don't think she's so good."
"Maybe that's it."

"That was a slave bracelet you gave me, wasn't it?"
"Yes, I had to slave for a year to buy it."

"What makes you think that mosquitoes are religious?"
"Well, first they sing over you and then they prey on you."

"Before I go away, I'd like to do something big and clean."
"Why don't you try washing an elephant?"

"What is the difference between vision and sight?"
"Well—remember those two girls we had last night?"
"Yes."
"The one I had was a vision and the one you had was a sight."

He was just a little piece of dandruff trying to get ahead.

"What's the difference between an elephant and a potfor?"
"What's a potfor?"
"To cook in, you dope."

"How can you make anti-freeze?"
"Hide her pajamas."

A bird in the hand is bad table manners.

"Is he a go-getter?"
"No, a have-it-brunger."

"Any news, girlie?"
"Listen—last night a section of the fire escape of the girls' dormitory fell down, and seven fellows were hurt."

"I've just been mistaken for the Prince of Wales."
"That's nothing. Yesterday a fellow walks up to me and says, 'Great God, is that you?'"

A taximeter is a thermometer that measures the fever of your pocketbook.

"What kind of oil do you use in your car, Joe?"
"Oh, I begin by telling them that I'm lonely."

A kibitzer is the unmarried part of the Siamese twins.

"Did you know that they can make shoes out of all kinds of skin?"
"How about banana skins?"
"They could make slippers out of them."

"Whatever becomes of all the brown autumn leaves?"
"Haven't you ever smoked a five-cent cigar?"

"Why are you rushing today?"
"I am trying to get something for my wife."
"Had any offers?"

"Which is the quickest way to the hospital?"
"Poking me in the back again with that cane of yours."

"Some men thirst after fame, some men thirst after love, and some after money."
"I know something that all men thirst after."
"What's that?"
"Salted peanuts."

"Thomas Smith is my name."
"I don't know you from Adam."
"You ought to. I dress differently."

"He reminds me of a wooden floor—full of dirty cracks!"

"No man can serve two masters."
"My brother tried it, and he was arrested for bigamy."

"What's the difference between a girl and a horse?"
"I don't know."
"You must have some great dates!"

"There's a man outside with a wooden leg named Smith."
"What's the name of his other leg?"

"The ancient Greeks often committed suicide."
"Them was the days. You can only do it once now."

It is better to keep your mouth shut and be thought a fool than to open it and remove all doubt.

"I hear they buried your janitor last week."
"Yes, they had to. He died."

"What time is it by your watch?"
"Quarter to."
"Quarter to what?"
"I don't know—times got so bad, I had to lay off one of my hands."

"In Siberia they don't hang a man with a wooden leg."
"Why not?"
"They use a rope."

"You remind me of George Washington."
"Why do I remind you of George Washington?"
"Because you're so different."

"I'm delighted to meet you. I've heard so much about you."
"You can't prove anything."

"He has a heart of gold ... yellow and hard."

"Have you a fairy godmother?"
"No, but I have an uncle I'm not so sure of."

"I'll never forget the time our ship was caught in a hurricane, we were grounded on the rocks, two miles from an isthmus."
"Isthmus? What is an isthmus?"
"An isthmus is a neck of dirt that water never touches."
"You've got an isthmus."

"Do you smoke?"
"Of course."
"How many cigarettes do you smoke a day?"
"Oh, any given number."

"The trouble with you," said a man in the audience to a public speaker, "is that you have a diarrhea of words and a constipation of ideas."

"Your daughter was talking of going to France this summer. Have you any objection?"
"No, certainly not! Let her talk!"

An adult is a person who has stopped growing on the ends and has started growing in the middle.

"Boy, how do you get to Macy's?"
"Aw, get the 'L' downtown."
"You little brat!"

A man is known by the company he keeps away from.

An executive is a guy who marries the boss's daughter.

"Do you know why the fisherman is the meanest of all men?"
"I certainly don't believe that."
"Well, they are because their business makes them sell-fish."

"My wife writes me that she is all unstrung—what shall I do?"
"Send her a wire."

"There's nothing worse than being old and bent."
"Yes, there is. Being young and broke."

"How can you get down off an elephant?"
"You climb down."
"Wrong!"
"You grease his sides and slide down."
"Wrong!"
"You take a ladder and get down."
"Wrong!"
"Well, you take the trunk line down!"
"All wrong! You don't get down off an elephant, you get it off a goose!"

"I was in a desperate predicament. I had to choose between shame or death."
"What did you choose, miss?"
"I'm not dead."

There's no denying the fact that honesty is the best poverty!

"All the men have gone on strike for shorter hours."
"I always said that sixty minutes was too long."

People who live in glass houses shouldn't.

A girl no longer marries a man for better or worse—she marries him for more or less.

Tobacco is found in many Southern states and in some cigars.

"What's a bigamist?"
"An optimist who is willing to take two chances."

"I would like to buy a double-barreled shotgun, please."
"Why, Mr. Jones—I didn't know you had a daughter!"

"What ho, Macodenos?"
"A fair maiden waits without."
"Without what?"
"Without food or clothing."
"Well, feed her and bring her in."

"Were you afraid to ask your father for money?"
"No, I stayed calm ... and collected."

"He died last year and left all he had to an orphan asylum."
"Indeed! That was nice of him. What did he leave?"
"His twelve children."

An echo is a hole in the wind.

"It is deeds, not words, that count."
"Not when you send a telegram."

"What is the difference between an elephant and a flea?"
"Well, an elephant can have fleas—but a flea can't have elephants."

"Do you know that sliced onion scattered around the room will absorb the odor of fresh paint?"
"Yes, and a broken neck will relieve a toothache."

"Can anyone tell me where the home of the swallow is?"
"The home of the swallow is in the stomach."

"When water becomes ice, what great change takes place?"
"The price!"

"Pop, what is a monologue?"
"A monologue is the conversation between a man and his wife."

Schoolboy's definition of water: a colorless liquid that turns black when you put your hands in it.

QUESTIONNAIRE

"How old is a person who is born in 1886?"
"Was it a man or a woman?"

"Now, dearie, what comes after 'g'?"
"Whiz."

"Billy, use the word 'notwithstanding' in a sentence."
"Father wore his trousers out, but notwithstanding."

"Can you give me a more elegant rendering of the sentence 'The sap rises'?"
"The boob gets out of bed."

"What is the name of the teeth we get last?"
"False teeth."

"If you should see a man hanging, what would you do?"
"Cut him down."
"Medically speaking."
"Cut him up!"

"If fifteen men ploughed a field in five hours, how long will thirty men take to plough the same field?"
"They couldn't do it."
"Why not?"
"Because the 15 men have already ploughed it."

"Where were you born?"
"Russia."
"What part?"
"All of me."
"Why did you leave Russia?"
"I couldn't bring it with me!"

"What are the five senses?"
"Nickels."

"Do you believe in capital punishment?"
"If it's not too severe."

"William, can you tell me who George Washington was?"
"Yes, ma'am, he was an American gen'ral."
"Quite right. And can you tell me what George Washington was remarkable for?"
"Yes, ma'am. He was remarkable because he was an American and told the truth."

"If a farmer raises 3,700 bushels of wheat and sells it for $2.50 per bushel, what will he get?"
"An automobile."

"Can you tell me one of the uses of cowhide?"
"Yes. It keeps the cow together."

(In mineralogy class) "Johnnie, tell me the name of the largest known diamond."
"The Ace."

"Tommy, what comes after 'O'?"
"Yeah!"

"Mom, where is the biggest dam in the world?"
"I don't know where it is now, son, but it was in the cellar last night when your father broke the only bottle of booze he had."

"Can you prove the proposition that the square of the hypotenuse of a right-angled triangle is equal to the sum of the squares of the other two sides?"
"I don't have to prove it. I admit it."

RADIO

"What kind of a radio have you got?"
"The railroad type; it whistles at every station."

"My radio is so small, when Amos 'n' Andy are on, I can only get Amos."

REAL ESTATE

"Why is he leaving for Florida?"
"He just got word that land was found on his property."

REDUCING

"What's the best exercise for reducing?"
"Just move the head slowly from right to left when asked to have a second helping."

"How come you're reducing?"
"Oh, to cut down on expanses."

"My, but you look thin today."
"Well, I ought to. I just lost 250 pounds."
"How is that?"
"My wife left me."

RELATIVITY

"What are diplomatic relations, Father?"
"There are no such people!"

"Is that chap Brown a relation of yours?"
"Only a distant relation."
"Very distant?"
"Oh yes. He's the eldest of 15 children, and I'm the youngest."

"Can you help me select a gift for a wealthy old aunt who is awfully weak and can hardly walk?"
"How about some floor wax?"

RELIGION

"William, what is the first thing your father says when he sits down at the table?"
"Go slow on the butter, kids, it's forty cents a pound."

"Why was Adam created first?"
"To give him a chance to say something, I guess."

"Is this the Salvation Army?"
"Yes."
"Do you save bad women?"
"Yes."
"Well, save a couple for me for Saturday night."

RESTAURANTS

"I'll take a half-dozen oysters on the half-shell."
"Sorry, sir, you'll have to wait a while."
"What's the matter?"
"Well, sir, we have the oysters, but we are a little short on shells, and I can't bring your order till that gent over there finishes."

"By Jove, I'm glad to see you back. Has the strike been settled?"
"What strike, sir?"
"Oh, come now. Where have you been since you took my order?"

"Look here, how long must I wait for the half-portion of duck I ordered?"
"Till somebody orders the other half."

"Waiter, bring me fried eggs and a kind word."
"Here are the eggs, sir."
"What's the kind word?"
"Don't eat the eggs."

(After 20 minutes) "Waiter, how about my order of fish?"
"The fish will be here in five minutes, sir."
(After 15 more minutes) "Well, waiter?"
"The fish will be here in a minute, sir."
"Tell me, waiter, what bait are you using?"

"You told me to go to that restaurant if I wanted some good roast beef."
"Well?"
"It was a bum steer."

"Waiter, this soup isn't fit for a pig."
"Just a minute, and I'll bring you some that is."

"I suppose, waiter, I can sit here till I starve."
"I'm afraid not, sir, we close at ten."

"Bring me one egg, not too soft, and not too hard, toast, not too hard, and coffee, not too weak and not too strong."
"Yes, sir. Any special pattern you'd like on the china?"

"What's good here?"
"Everything, sir."
"Everything? Have it served at once."
"Hash for one!"

A waiter brings a patron a very tiny portion and the price is terribly high. The patron examines the small dish, nods his head approvingly, and says, "That's what I want. Bring me an order of that."

"You certainly gave that cloak room attendant a big tip."
"Well, he gave me a darn good coat!"

"Do you want a steak for a dollar, or a dollar and a half?"
"What's the difference?"
"For a dollar and a half you get a sharp knife."

"Waiter, my bill."
"What did you have, sir?"
"I don't know."
"You don't know?"
"No—I ordered a tender steak."

"I want a turkey sandwich."
"We ain't got no turkey."
"All right—give me a chicken sandwich then."
"Don't be a fool. If we had chicken, wouldn't I have given you a turkey sandwich?"

"Sir, about that steak you ordered 20 minutes ago. How'd you like it?"
"Very much indeed."

"They say that waiters can always size a man up."
"I suppose they measure him from tip to tip."

"Waiter, take this coffee away. It's like mud."
"Well, it was ground this morning."

"Waiter, this steak is like leather and this knife is dull."
"You must strop the knife on the steak."

"There's a fly in my coffee!"
"Come on, he didn't drink *that* much."

"Have you got any wild rabbit?"
"No, but we can get one and irritate it for you."

"The soup is excellent tonight, sir."
"Did you make it?"
"I had a finger in it."

"How did you find the steak, sir?"
"Oh, I just lifted up a green pea and there it was!"

RETORTS

"Sweets to the sweet."
"Thank you. Won't you have some nuts?"

"Does your watch tell you the time?"
"No, I have to look at it."

"Do boats like this sink often?"
"No, only once."

"What are spectacles?"
"Spectacles are glasses which people look through."
"If you looked through a window, would you call that a spectacle?"
"It all depends on what you saw."

"Mommy, why do ducks and geese fly north in the winter?"
"Because it's too far to walk."

"Where were you born?"
"Glasgow."
"Glasgow! What for?"
"I wanted to be near my mother."

"Where are you going, daughter?"
"To get water."
"In your nightgown?"
"No, in this glass."

"We want to buy a ticket."
"But there are two of you."
"We're half-sisters. Add it up."

"Do you know smoking shortens your life?"
"Well, I've smoked for sixty years and I'm eighty now."
"See? If you hadn't smoked, you'd be ninety by now."

"I passed your place yesterday."
"Thanks."

"Do you drink?"
"That's my business."
"Have you any other business?"

"You speak foolishly."
"So that you can understand me."

"Did he have a habit of singing to himself when he was alone?"
"I don't know, I wasn't with him when he was alone."

"Hey, there were three pints of liquor in my trunk last night, and now there's only one. What's the big idea?"
"Well, it was dark and I didn't see the third one."

"My parents tried hard to keep me from becoming an artist."
"I congratulate them on their success."

ROBBERY

"A crook hid in my stove, and when I lifted my revolver, he ran out."
"Did you shoot him?"
"No, he was out of my range."

"I held up an author last night."
"How much did you get?"
"Get? It cost me a dollar."

"Get out of here. I'm workin' this floor."
"G'wan! This is my story and I'll stick to it."

"Conductor, I've been robbed. The fellow sitting in the seat next to me stole my pocketbook when we went through the tunnel. I had it in my stocking."
"Why did you let him?"
"How did I know he was after my money?"

"Where have you been?"
"Robbing a politician's house."
"Did you lose anything?"

"What became of the man who stole the calendar?"
"He got twelve months."

"Did you hear about the burglar breaking into our house?"
"What did he get?"
"Nothing but practice."

"You say you're looking for a cashier? I thought you hired one last week?"
"I did; that's the one I'm looking for."

STOREKEEPERS

"How much are those tomatoes?"
"Seven cents a pound."
"Did you raise them yourself?"
"Yes—they were five cents yesterday."

TAILORS

"I've brought that last pair of trousers back to be re-seated. You know, I sit a lot."
"Fine. And I hope you brought the bill in to be receipted—you know, I've stood a lot."

"That coat is not a very good fit, Einstein."
"Vell, vat do you expect for fife dollars? An attack of epilepsy?"

TELEPHONES

"Hello, is this the beauty shop?"
"Yes."
"Well, send one over, will you?"

"I say, my phone hasn't been working for a month and you paid no attention to my letter of complaint."
"We did—we rang you up to ask what was wrong and we got no answer."

"Who is that shouting?"
"That's Mr. Hill talking to Edinburgh."
"Then tell him to use the telephone!"

"Excuse me, sir, but I'm in a hurry. You've had that phone twenty minutes and haven't said a word."
"I'm talking to my wife."

THEATRE

"Did the new play have a happy ending?"
"Sure. Everybody was glad when it was over."

"What are the prices of the seats?"
"Orchestra seats five dollars, balcony seats two and a half dollars, and programs a dime."
"That's fine—I'll sit on a program."

"They advertised a chorus of seventy … and they looked it."

"Why were you weeping in the picture show?"
"Well, it was a moving picture."

"How far down do you want to sit, sir?"
"Why, all the way down, of course."

TRAINS

"The 12:50 is a very hard train to catch because it is 10 to 1 if you catch it."

"I have to go to Philadelphia."
"Is that a complaint or do you want a ticket?"

TRAVEL

"Don't you think that travel brings out all there is in one?"
"Yes. If it's ocean travel."

"I noticed you got up in the subway to give your seat to a woman."
"Since childhood I have always respected a woman with a strap in her hand."

"Where is the American section in Paris?"
"The first ten rows at the Folies Bergere."

TWINS

"How is it that you have a picture of only one of the twins?"
"They both look exactly alike, so what's the difference?"

"She had triplets and, a few weeks later, she had twins."
"How is that possible?"
"One of the triplets died."

WOMEN

There was a woman who got so tired she could hardly keep her mouth open.

"What are you doing at this party?"
"I'm looking for my husband."
"What's his name?"
"I don't know yet."

"My wife doesn't understand me. Does yours?"
"I don't know—I never heard her mention your name."

"What we want is a night watchman who'll watch, alert and ready, for the slightest noise or indication of burglars. Somebody who can sleep with one eye and both ears open, and is not afraid to tackle anything."
"I see, sir. I'll send my wife around."

"Should I take my wife to a prizefight?"
"No. Too much education for a woman is a dangerous thing."

"Last night when I arrived home my wife had my chair drawn up before the fire, my slippers ready for me to put on, my pipe—"
"How did you like her new hat?"

"I hear Dora was married last night."
"Yeah? Who gave the bride away?"
"I could have, but I kept my mouth shut."

"Why so sad?"
"I said something to my wife and she wouldn't speak to me for a week."
"That's too bad. When did that happen?"
"About a month ago."
"Well, why so sad now?"
"I've forgotten what I said."

A Morman was very ill. One of his wives intercepted the doctor and said, "Oh doctor, is my husband very sick?"
"Yes, madam, I'm afraid he is."
"Do you think I ought to go to his bedside?"
"I think you should, but you'd better hurry. All the best places are taken."

"Where did your wife get that stunning new hat?"
"She gave it to me for my birthday."

"You say your wife never wants credit for anything she does?"
"No, she wants cash."

"Lots of girls use dumbbells to get color in their cheeks."
"Yes, and lots of girls use color in their cheeks to get dumbbells."

"Did you buy that ninety-dollar hat you were raving over?"
"Yes."
"What does your husband think of it?"
"He raved over it, too."

"Why does a woman keep her money in her stocking instead of a bank?"
"It draws more interest there."

"There's a race of wild women there who have no mouths and can't talk."
"Probably that's what makes them wild."

"What's the difference between Jean Harlow and the Panama Canal?"
"The Panama Canal is a busy ditch!"

"She is going to marry an x-ray specialist."
"He's the only one who could see anything in her."

Christmas is the time when a girl forgets her past, ignores her future and thinks of nothing but the present.

"Now, miss, what gear were you in at the time of the accident?"
"Oh—I had on a black beret—tan shoes—and a sports dress—"

When a man has a birthday, he takes a day off. When a woman has a birthday, she takes a year off.

"How do they catch lunatics, Father?"
"With face powder, lipstick and clothes."

"Is the bookkeeper modest?"
"Modest! Say, that girl wouldn't even do improper fractions."

"She's a decided blonde, isn't she?"
"Yeah, but she only decided recently."

A beautician says nothing is less attractive than an elderly woman with bleached hair. Only the good dye young, it seems.

"I don't intend to be married until after I'm thirty."
"I don't intend to be thirty until after I'm married."

"Who was that peach I saw you with last night?"
"That was no peach, that was a grapefruit."
"Why grapefruit?"
"When I squeezed her, she hit me in the eye."

"That dame's fast."
"That so?"
"Yes, she made six laps in one night."

"I can't take my girl to a Jewish café."
"Why not?"
"She eats like a pig!"

"Now, you pride yourself on being able to judge a woman's character by her clothes. Now, what would be your opinion on my sister over there?"
"Insufficient evidence."

A man always chases a woman until she catches him.

"Who was that blonde you were out with Wednesday and Thursday?"
"She was the brunette I was out with Monday and Tuesday."

"I see where they found the two-thousand-year-old skull of a woman."
"How can they tell the skull was a woman's after two thousand years?"
"The mouth was open."

"She didn't give her husband a moment's rest
until he bought her a motor car."
"I didn't know auto-suggestion really worked."

"They say she is very musical."
"So she is. She has a sharp tongue, a flat nose and a natural voice."

"What are the ten best years of a woman's life?"
"From twenty-eight to thirty."

"There were two men standing outside your window while you were
   dressing, ma'am."
"That's nothing. You should have seen the crowd when I was younger."

"Where does Marie get her good looks?"
"From her dad."
"Handsome man, eh?"
"No, druggist."

"Do you know that lady we just passed?"
"Indeed I do. I used to pay that woman compliments five years ago."
"And now?"
"Now I pay her alimony."

"Women are the most biased creatures I have ever seen."
"Why so?"
"All they ever say is 'Bias this and bias that.'"

WRITERS

"This is certainly well written, but we only accept work from authors with well-known names."
"That's great—my name's Smith!"

"Have you submitted this poem anywhere else?"
"No, sir."
"Then where did you get that black eye?"

"When does an author become a classic?"
"When nobody reads him and everybody says they do."

"Have you seen the new play I wrote about the couple who were always quarreling?"
"No, but I heard you and your wife rehearsing it."

"Once I got a dollar a word."
"Gwan! What for?"
"Talking back to the judge."

"John, why is it your composition on milk only covers a half page when you were told to make it two pages long?"
"I was writing about condensed milk."

"Did you know that I've taken up short-story writing as a profession?"
"Sold anything?"
"Yes—my watch, my mandolin and my coat!"

"I don't know how to kill off my chief character."
"Read your play to him."

"Milton was a great poet who wrote 'Paradise Lost,' then his wife died and he wrote 'Paradise Regained.'"

"I get twenty cents a word for my stuff. I'm a word painter."
"I get two dollars a word for mine. I'm a sign painter."

"For ten long, lean years I've been changing this drama—a word here, a line there, working on it till my fingers are cramped, and my body is weary from the toll."
"Too bad, too bad. All work and no play."

"Dash it, I can't find that sonnet anywhere. Sam must have thrown it into the fire."
"Don't be silly, dear. The child can't read."

"Who is the hero of your new story?"
"My publisher."

www.ingramcontent.com/pod-product-compliance
Lightning Source LLC
Chambersburg PA
CBHW070908160426
43193CB00011B/1406